To: Charlie          Dec. 2010

From: Priscilla with Love

*The Quotable*

# AMERICAN
# CIVIL WAR

*The Quotable*

# AMERICAN
# CIVIL WAR

## IAIN C. MARTIN

THE LYONS PRESS
Guilford, Connecticut
*An imprint of The Globe Pequot Press*

The Lyons Press is an imprint of
The Globe Pequot Press

Text design by Sheryl P. Kober

Library of Congress Cataloging-in-Publication Data
is available on file.

ISBN 978-1-59921-340-8

Printed in the United States of America

10 9 8 7 6 5 4 3 2 1

# CONTENTS

"The American Civil War—April to April, Sumter to Appomattox, 1861 to 1865—pervades the national conscience . . . It makes a great story. I know of none since the *Iliad* that rivals it either in drama or in pathos."

—SHELBY FOOTE

# Introduction

AT THE AGE OF FIFTEEN I MADE MY FIRST
visit to Gettysburg National Military Park. The natural beauty
and peacefulness of the landscape, not so different from my
upstate New York homeland, struck me right away. The rolling wooded hills and gentle farmlands made it hard to envision
the greatest battle ever fought in North America raged there
over three days in July 1863. Yet the weight of history whis-
pers from every corner of Gettysburg, and as I walked along
Cemetery Ridge, stood at the marker where the 20th Maine
held the line at Little Round Top, or gazed eastward from Seminary Ridge upon that long open mile toward the Emmitsburg
Road, I began to understand the true meaning of courage. Years
later I would discover the writings of Joshua L. Chamberlain:
"In great deeds something abides. On great fields something
stays. Forms change and pass; bodies disappear, but spirits linger, to consecrate ground for the vision-place of souls." It was a

place and time when I knew what it meant to be an American; that the Civil War was an event that had shaped our every step forward as a nation.

The United States in the spring of 1861 was truly a divided country. While the northern states continued to develop heavy industries and a bustling international commerce, the southern states remained an agrarian society where "king cotton" fueled the industrial might of English textiles. Slave labor was not only a basis of this economy, but a way of life deeply embedded in southern culture under a racial hierarchy where the white race stood supreme. South Carolina Senator James Henry Hammond pronounced before the United States Senate in 1858, "Our slaves are black, of another and inferior race. The status in which we have placed them is an elevation. They are elevated from the condition in which God first created them, by being made our slaves." Under this system, the nearly four million slaves of the southern population made a powerful economic, social, and political interest. Abraham Lincoln referred to this in his 1865 Inaugural Address, "One eighth of the whole population were colored slaves, not distributed generally over the Union, but localized in the Southern part of it. These slaves constituted a peculiar and powerful interest. All knew that this interest was, somehow, the cause of the war."

The westward expansion of slavery was the key issue that moved the nation toward war by 1860. Abraham Lincoln and the Republican Party sought to restrict slavery to the states where it already existed. Lincoln proclaimed he had no legal right to seek an end to slavery if he became president. His moral convictions on the slavery question, however, were well known. In 1854 he declared in Illinois, "Near eighty years ago we began by declaring that all men are created equal; but now from that beginning we have run down to the other declaration, that for *some* men to enslave others is a 'sacred right of self-government.' These principles cannot stand together. They are as opposite as God and Mammon; and whoever holds to the one must despise the other." The southern people felt their way of life threatened by the possibility that an end to slavery would be forced upon them by a northern majority if Lincoln was elected president.

Following Lincoln's confirmation as president elect in November 1860, South Carolina moved to secede from the Union with a unanimous vote on December 20, 1860. During the next two months, ordinances of secession were adopted by the states of Mississippi, Florida, Alabama, Georgia, Louisiana, and Texas. By February 1861, the seceding states formed the Confederacy under a provisional constitution with Jefferson Davis as president and Alexander Hamilton Stephens as vice president. Eleven federal forts and arsenals were seized from South Carolina to Texas, with Fort Sumter at Charleston taking the center stage for what became the powder keg's spark. Jefferson Davis proclaimed as much during his inaugural speech on February 18, "The time for compromise has now passed, and the South is determined to maintain her position, and make all who oppose her smell Southern powder and feel Southern steel."

In Lincoln's inaugural address on March 4, the question of civil war was squarely placed in the hands of the Confederacy, yet he appealed for conciliation: "We are not enemies, but friends. We must not be enemies. Though passion may have strained it must not break our bonds of affection. The mystic chords of memory, stretching from every battlefield and patriot grave to every living heart and hearthstone all over this broad land, will yet swell the chorus of the Union, when again touched, as surely they will be, by the better angels of our nature." When Lincoln sent a fleet of ships to supply Fort Sumter soon afterward, Confederate artillery opened fire, forcing its surrender on April 13. Three days later Lincoln announced that an insurrection had occurred, and he called for volunteers. Virginia would join the Confederacy the same month, and Arkansas, Tennessee, and North Carolina in May. Both North and South prepared for war.

What followed was a four-year struggle that raged not only between North and South, but between families—brothers against brothers, fathers against sons. The West Point classes were divided as many officers resigned their commissions to return to their southern states and fight for the Confederacy. Robert E. Lee, after refusing the command of the Union armies, returned to his native Virginia even though he opposed the war. He wrote to his son, "I can anticipate no greater calamity for the country than the dissolution of the Union. It would be an accumulation of all the evils we complain of, and I am willing to sacrifice everything but honor for its preservation." In the Lincoln family, six of Mary Todd's close relatives all fought for the Confederacy, while her southern kin labeled her a traitor. It was a war that would literally tear the nation apart, inflicting more casualties than all of America's previous wars combined.

The catastrophic horrors of the Civil War came in part from both the success and failure of modern science. Where the advancement of weaponry had more than doubled the range and firepower of artillery and firearms, the medical sciences failed to match the needs of the soldiers. Far more men would die of disease and infection during the war than combat. Thousands of young men, most away from home for the first time and hailing from distant farmlands, would travel to military camps and into contact with afflictions to which they had little to no immunity. The high-caliber, low-muzzle velocity weapons of the era often shattered bones so that only amputation was possible to save a man's life. Due to the lack of knowledge about the causes of infection and without the possibility of blood transfusions, doctors could only save about half those who underwent the loss of an arm or leg.

Military leaders also failed to take into account their tactics were based upon the Napoleonic wars from the turn of the century when the smooth bore musket was the standard firearm. Men were massed shoulder to shoulder and moved to within a hundred yards of an enemy position before advancing with bayonets to break the opposing line. The evolution of the rifled musket and minie ball pushed the accurate range of the average soldier from fifty yards to two hundred and fifty yards. An enemy line could be put under deadly fire en masse at half a mile. Likewise, the advancement of rifled artillery and ammunition for cannon made a frontal assault a decidedly lethal affair, as witnessed on countless battlefields throughout the Civil War. A Union officer recalled the carnage at Antietam, "Every stalk of corn in the northern and greater part of the field was cut as closely as could have been done with a knife, and the slain lay in rows precisely as they stood in their ranks a few minutes before."

Anyone looking for the origins of mechanized warfare need only to consider the tens of thousands slain and the trenches of Petersburg at the end of the Civil War to foresee what would come a half-century later in the First World War. As historian Shelby Foote so aptly noted, the American Civil War was the last romantic and first modern war.

Yet the Civil War would give rise to our greatest president since Washington—Abraham Lincoln, who would change the focus of the war to the abolition of slavery with the Emancipation Proclamation in September 1862. Although the proclamation only addressed slavery within the states under rebellion, it would set in motion the ratification of the 13th Amendment in December 1865 abolishing slavery from the United States forever. In his greatest speech at Gettysburg, in November 1863, Lincoln defined this change in the war, "that from these honored dead we take increased devotion to that cause for which they gave the last full measure of devotion—that we here highly resolve that these dead shall not have died in vain—that this nation, under God, shall have a new birth of freedom—and that government of the people, by the people, for the people, shall not perish from the earth."

The war would continue for another seventeen months. In the end Lincoln would survive just long enough to see his great work nearly completed when General Robert E. Lee surrendered his Army of Northern Virginia to Lieutenant General Ulysses S. Grant at Appomattox, Virginia, on April 9, 1865. A few days earlier, Lincoln had telegrammed General Grant, "I want no one punished. Treat them liberally all around. We want those people to return to their allegiance to the Union and submit to the laws." It set the tone for what would become a merciful and conciliatory peace. Confederate Major General John B. Gordon wrote years later, "The meeting of Lee and Grant at Appomattox was the momentous epoch of the century. It marked greater changes, uprooted a grander and nobler civilization, and, in the emancipation of one race and the impoverishment of another, it involved vaster consequences than had ever followed the fall of a dynasty or the wreck of an empire." Lincoln would live until April 14, where his fate took him to Ford's Theatre in Washington, D.C. and his assassination at the hand of John Wilkes Booth.

In the end, the Civil War is at the heart of the American story; a continuation of events of 1776, when it was declared that all men are created equal; a testament to where we have been and who we are as a free people today. It is a story that all Americans share, no matter what their ancestry or heritage. It was the events at Gettysburg in July 1863 and Lincoln's immortal dedication to the fallen in November that year that we look back upon as the pinnacle of what the war meant for all Americans; the Confederacy, at the edge of victory, fighting courageously for the Southern cause; the Union defending the Republic from breaking apart and to end the scourge of slavery. The Civil War forged, through fire and steel, the country as we understand it today.

*The Quotable American Civil War* is a collection of the most important, most eloquent, and memorable words from that bygone era. This is by no means a complete collection, but it represents as many of the participants and events as possible.

The quotes are collected from eyewitness accounts, letters, diaries, reports, songs and poems, from people in all walks of life. They represent the heart and soul of the American experience from the Civil War. Walt Whitman wrote in 1882, "The real war will never get in the books. And so goodbye to the war." By collecting these original, first-person narratives and quotes, I hope to have come as close as possible to bringing the Civil War back to readers.

Iain C. Martin
February 2008

EDITOR'S NOTE: *Whenever possible I have cited where a selection originated. Any errors in its presentation are strictly my own. A special thank you to Lyons Press editor Tom McCarthy for his support for this book, and to my father, Blair R. Martin.*

# ONE

# *A* House
# Divided

WHEN IN THE COURSE OF HUMAN EVENTS IT becomes necessary for one people to dissolve the political bonds which have connected them with another, and to assume among the powers of the earth, the separate and equal status to which the laws of nature and nature's God entitles them a decent respect for the opinions of mankind requires that they should declare the causes which impel them to the separation.

—DECLARATION OF INDEPENDENCE, JULY 4, 1776

The future inhabitants of the Atlantic and Mississippi states will be our sons. We think we see their happiness in their union, and we wish it. Events may prove otherwise; and if they see their interest in separating why should we take sides? *God bless them both, and keep them in union if it be for their good, but separate them if it be better.*

—THOMAS JEFFERSON,
*letter to John C. Breckenridge, August 1803*

*The Union was formed by the voluntary agreement of the States; and these, in uniting together, have not forfeited their Nationality, nor have they been reduced to the condition of one and the same people. If one of the States chose to withdraw its name from the contract, it would be difficult to disprove its right of doing so.*

—ALEXIS DE TOCQUEVILLE,
*Democracy in America, 1835*

Near eighty years ago we began by declaring that all men are created equal; but now from that beginning we have run down to the other declaration, that for *some* men to enslave others is a "sacred right of self-government." These principles cannot stand together. They are as opposite as God and Mammon; and whoever holds to the one must despise the other.

—Abraham Lincoln,
*speech at Peoria, Illinois, October 16, 1854*

*A house divided against itself cannot stand.*

I believe this government cannot endure, permanently half *slave* and half *free*.

I do not expect the Union to be *dissolved*—I do not expect the house to *fall*—but I *do* expect it will cease to be divided.

*It will become* all *one thing or* all *the other.*

—ABRAHAM LINCOLN,
*acceptance speech for U.S. Senate,*
*Republican State Convention,*
*Springfield, Illinois, June 16, 1858*

# WHAT WOULD HAPPEN IF NO COTTON WAS FURNISHED FOR THREE YEARS?

*I will not stop to depict what every one can imagine, but this is certain: England would topple headlong and carry the whole civilized world with her, save the South. No, you dare not make war on cotton. No power on earth dares to make war upon it.*

## *Cotton is king.*

—JAMES HENRY HAMMOND,
SPEECH BEFORE THE
UNITED STATES SENATE,
MARCH 4, 1858

NOW, MY COUNTRYMEN, if you have been taught doctrines conflicting with the great landmarks of the Declaration of Independence; if you have listened to suggestions which would take away from its grandeur, and mutilate the fair symmetry of its proportions; if you have been inclined to believe that all men are not created equal in those inalienable rights enumerated by our chart of liberty, let me entreat you to come back. Return to the fountain whose waters spring close by the blood of the Revolution.

—ABRAHAM LINCOLN, *speech at Lewistown, Illinois, August 17, 1858*

*Now, if it is deemed necessary that I should forfeit my life for the furtherance of the ends of justice, and mingle my blood further with the blood of my children and with the blood of millions in this slave country whose rights are disregarded by wicked, cruel, and unjust enactment's—I submit; so let it be done.*

—JOHN BROWN,
*statement at his sentencing on November 2, 1859*

# The fight must go on.

*The cause of civil liberty must not be surrendered at the end of one or even, one hundred defeats. Douglas had the ingenuity to be supported in the late contest both as the best means to break down, and to uphold the Slave interest. No ingenuity can keep those antagonistic elements in harmony long.*

*Another explosion will soon come.*

—Abraham Lincoln,
letter to Henry Asbury, November 19, 1858

THIS WILL BE A GREAT DAY IN OUR HISTORY; the date of a New Revolution—quite as much needed as the old one. Even now as I write they are leading old John Brown to execution in Virginia for attempting to rescue slaves! This is sowing the wind to reap the whirlwind which will come soon!

—HENRY WADSWORTH LONGFELLOW, *commenting on the execution of John Brown on December 2, 1859*

I JOHN BROWN am now quite certain that the crimes of this guilty land will never be purged away but with blood.

—JOHN BROWN, *last words written before his execution, December 2, 1859*

Neither let us be slandered from our duty by false accusations against us, nor frightened from it by menaces of destruction to the Government nor of dungeons to ourselves. *Let us have faith that right makes might, and in that faith, let us, to the end, dare to do our duty as we understand it.*

—Abraham Lincoln,
*speech at Cooper's Union, New York City, February 27, 1860*

*T*he fact is that our Union rests upon public opinion and can never be cemented by the blood of its citizens shed in civil war. If it cannot live in the affections of the people, it must one day perish. Congress possesses many means of preserving it by conciliation, but the sword was not placed in their hand to preserve it by force.

—President James Buchanan,
*state of the union address, December 4, 1860*

## I KNOW THERE IS A GOD, AND THAT HE HATES INJUSTICE AND SLAVERY.

*I see the storm coming, and I know that His hand is in it. If He has a place and work for me, and I think He has, I believe I'm ready.* *I am nothing, but Truth is everything.*

—ABRAHAM LINCOLN, 1860

Our government is an agency of delegated and strictly limited powers. *Its founders did not look to its preservation by force but the chain they wove to bind these States together was one of love and mutual good offices.*

—U.S. SENATOR JEFFERSON DAVIS, *speech to the U.S. Senate, December 10, 1860*

SHOULD THE STEP BE TAKEN which is now threatened, we shall have no other alternative: we must fight. But do not think that all Christian people of the land could be induced to unite in prayer, to avert so great an evil? It seems to me that if they would unite in prayer, war might be prevented and peace preserved.

—THOMAS J. JACKSON,
*letter to a minister friend, 1860*

*If the cotton states shall become satisfied that they can do better out of the Union than in it, we insist on letting them go in peace. . . . We hope never to live in a Republic whereof one section is pinned to another by bayonets.*

—HORACE GREELEY,
*editorial,* New York Tribune, *December 17, 1860*

YOU PEOPLE OF THE SOUTH DON'T KNOW what you are doing. This country will be drenched in blood, and God only knows how it will end. It is all folly, madness, a crime against civilization! You people speak so lightly of war; you don't know what you're talking about *War is a terrible thing!*

—U.S. BRIGADIER GENERAL
WILLIAM TECUMSEH SHERMAN,
*comment to friend, Professor David F. Boyd*
*of Virginia, December 24, 1860, quoted by Shelby Foote,*
The Civil War, *vol. 1, 1958*

## Some of you laugh

to scorn the idea of bloodshed as the result of secession, but let me tell you what is coming... After the sacrifice of countless millions of treasure and hundreds of thousands of lives you may win Southern independence, but I doubt it. The North is determined to preserve this Union. They are not a fiery, impulsive people as you are, for they live in colder climates. But when they begin to move in a given direction, they move with the steady momentum and perseverance of a mighty avalanche.

—Texas Governor Sam Houston, 1860

I think I see in the future a gory head rise above our horizon. Its name is Civil War. Already I can see the prints of his bloody fingers upon our lintels and doorposts. THE VISION SICKENS ME ALREADY.

—THOMAS READE ROOTES COBB,
*speech in Milledgeville, Georgia, November 12, 1860*

IF THE GENERAL GOVERNMENT should persist in the measures now threatened, there must be *war.* It is painful to discover with what unconcern they speak of war, and threaten it. They do not know the horrors. I have seen enough of it to make me look upon it as the sum of all evils.

—PROFESSOR THOMAS J. JACKSON,
*Virginia Military Institute, letter to
Reverend William White, December 19, 1860*

*D*o the people of the South really entertain fears that a Republican administration would, directly, or indirectly, interfere with their slaves, or with them, about their slaves? If they do, I wish to assure you, as once a friend, and still, I hope, not an enemy, that there is no cause for such fears. The South would be in no more danger in this respect, than it was in the days of Washington. I suppose, however, this does not meet the case. You think slavery is right, and ought to be extended; while we think it is wrong and ought to be restricted. That I suppose is the rub. It certainly is the only substantial difference between us.

—ABRAHAM LINCOLN,
*letter to Alexander Stephens, December 22, 1860*

I CAN ANTICIPATE NO GREATER CALAMITY for the country than the dissolution of the Union. It would be an accumulation of all the evils we complain of, and I am willing to sacrifice everything but honor for its preservation.

—U.S. COLONEL ROBERT E. LEE,
*letter to his son Custis, January 23, 1861*

IF WE DO NOT MAKE COMMON cause to save the good old ship of the Union on this voyage, nobody will have a chance to pilot her on another voyage.

—ABRAHAM LINCOLN,
*Address, Cleveland, Ohio,*
*February 15, 1861*

The great principle embodied by Jefferson in the Declaration is that "governments derive their just power from the consent of the governed" so if the Southern states want to secede they have a clear right to do so. *If a tyrannical government justified the Revolution of 1776, we do not see why it would not justify the secession of five millions of Southrons from the Federal Union in 1861.*

—HORACE GREELEY,
*editorial,* New York Tribune,
*February 18, 1861*

*There is really no crisis except an artificial one . . .*
*If the great American people will only keep their temper,*
*on both sides of the line, the trouble will come to an end.*

—ABRAHAM LINCOLN,
COMMENT MADE PRIOR TO HIS INAUGURATION, FEBRUARY 15, 1861

*All that the South has ever desired is that the Union of fore fathers should be preserved.*

—C.S. GENERAL ROBERT E. LEE

THE TIME FOR COMPROMISE HAS NOW PASSED, and the South is determined to maintain her position, and make all who oppose her smell Southern powder and feel Southern steel.

—C.S. PRESIDENT JEFFERSON DAVIS,
*inaugural speech, February 18, 1861*

In *your hands,* my dissatisfied fellow countrymen, and not in *mine* is the momentous issue of civil war. The government will not assail you. You can have no conflict without being yourselves the aggressors. You have no oath registered in heaven to destroy the government, while I have the most solemn one to "preserve, protect and defend" it.

WE ARE NOT ENEMIES, BUT FRIENDS. We must not be enemies. Though passion may have strained it must not break our bonds of affection. The mystic chords of memory, stretching from every battlefield and patriot grave to every living heart and hearthstone all over this broad land, will yet swell the chorus of the Union, when again touched, as surely they will be, by the better angels of our nature.

—U.S. PRESIDENT ABRAHAM LINCOLN,
*March 4, 1861, First Inaugural Address*

THE MAN DOES NOT LIVE WHO IS MORE devoted to peace than I am. None who would do more to preserve it. But it many be necessary to put the foot down firmly.

—PRESIDENT ABRAHAM LINCOLN,
*speech to the New Jersey Senate, February 21, 1861*

THE STATES HAVE their status in the Union, and they have no other legal status. If they break from this they can only do so against law and by revolution.

—ABRAHAM LINCOLN,
*Message to Congress in Special Session, July 4, 1861*

*The time for war has not yet come, but it will come, and that soon; and when it does come, my advice is to draw the sword and throw away the scabbard.*

—C.S. Lieutenant General Thomas J. Jackson, *speech to the cadets at the Virginia Military Institute, April 13, 1861*

With all my devotion to the Union and the feeling of loyalty and duty of an American citizen, I have not been able to make up my mind to raise my hand against my relatives, my children, my home. *I have, therefore, resigned my commission in the Army.*

—Robert E. Lee, *letter to his sister, Mrs. Anne Marshall, April 20, 1861*

*South Carolina is too small for a republic and too large for an insane asylum.*

—CONFEDERATE JAMES PETIGRU,
*upon hearing of South Carolina's secession*

*We feel that our cause is just and holy;* we protest solemnly in the face of mankind that we desire peace at any sacrifice save that of honor and independence; we seek no conquest, no aggrandizement, no concession of any kind from the States with which we were lately confederated; all we ask is to be let alone; that those who never held power over us shall not now attempt our subjugation by arms. *This we will, this we must, resist to the direst extremity.*

—C.S. PRESIDENT JEFFERSON DAVIS,
*"Message on Constitutional Ratification" to the Provisional Congress of the Confederate States of America, Montgomery, Alabama, April 29, 1861*

# I am with the South in life or in death, in victory or in defeat ...

*I believe the North is about to wage a brutal and unholy war on a people who have done them no wrong, in violation of the Constitution and the fundamental principles of government. They no longer acknowledge that all government derives its validity from the consent of the governed. They are about to invade our peaceful homes, destroy our property, and inaugurate a servile insurrection, murder our men and dishonor our women.*

*We propose no invasion of the North, no attack on them, and only ask to be left alone.*

—C.S. Major General Patrick Cleburne,
May 1861

Two

*On*

Slavery

*I think we must get rid of slavery,*
*or we must get rid of freedom.*

—RALPH WALDO EMERSON

GO SEARCH WHERE YOU WILL, roam through all the monarchies and despotisms of the Old World, travel through South America, search out every abuse and when you have found the last, lay your facts by the side of the everyday practices of this nation, and you will say with me that, for revolting barbarity and shameless hypocrisy, America reigns without a rival.

—FREDERICK DOUGLASS,
*Rochester, New York, July 4, 1852*

# What, to the American slave, is your 4th of July?

*I answer; a day that reveals to him, more than all other days in the year, the gross injustice and cruelty to which he is the constant victim . . .*

*There is not a nation on the earth guilty of practices more shocking and bloody than are the people of the United States, at this very hour.*

—Frederick Douglass, Rochester, New York, July 4, 1852

*When the white man governs himself that is self-government; but when he governs himself and also governs another man, that is more than self-government—that is despotism.*

—ABRAHAM LINCOLN,
*speech at Peoria, Illinois,*
*October 16, 1854*

*I appear this evening as a thief and a robber.* I stole this head, these limbs, this body from my master, and ran off with them.

—FREDERICK DOUGLASS

As I would not be a *slave*, so I would not be a *master*.
This expresses my idea of democracy.
*Whatever differs from this, to the extent of
the difference, is not democracy.*

—Abraham Lincoln,
*August 1858*

THE COMPACT
which exists between the North and the South is a
covenant with death and an agreement with hell.

—William Lloyd Garrison

IN THIS ENLIGHTENED AGE, THERE ARE FEW
I believe, but what will acknowledge, that slavery as an
institution, is a moral and political evil in any Country. . . .
I think it however a greater evil to the white man than to
the black race, and while my feelings are strongly enlisted
in behalf of the latter, my sympathies are more strong for
the former. The blacks are immeasurably better off here
than in Africa, morally, socially and physically. The painful discipline they are undergoing, is necessary for their
instruction as a race, and I hope will prepare and lead them
to better things. How long their subjugation may be necessary is known and ordered by a wise Merciful Providence.

—U.S. Lieutenant Colonel Robert E. Lee,
*letter to his wife, Mary, December 27, 1856*

*If I thought this war was to abolish slavery,*
*I would resign my commission, and offer my sword*
*to the other side.*

—ULYSSES S. GRANT

IT IS NOT TRUE THAT OUR FATHERS, AS JUDGE DOUGLAS ASSUMES, MADE THIS GOVERNMENT PART SLAVE AND PART FREE.

*. . . He assumes that slavery is a rightful thing within itself—was introduced by the framers of the Constitution. The exact truth is that they found the institution existing among us, and they left it as they found it. But in making the government they left this institution with many clear marks of disapprobation upon it.*

*They found slavery among them and they left it among them because of the difficulty—the absolute impossibility of its immediate removal.*

—ABRAHAM LINCOLN,
seventh debate with Stephen Douglas,
Alton, Illinois, October 15, 1858

MR. LINCOLN, FOLLOWING THE EXAMPLE and lead of all the little Abolition orators, who go around and lecture in the basements of schools and churches, reads from the Declaration of Independence, that all men were created equal, and then asks, how can you deprive a negro of that equality which God and the Declaration of Independence awards to him? . . . He holds that the negro was born his equal and yours, and that he was endowed with equality by the Almighty, and that no human law can deprive him of these rights which were guarantied to him by the Supreme ruler of the Universe. Now, I do not believe that the Almighty ever intended the negro to be the equal of the white man . . . He belongs to an inferior race, and must always occupy an inferior position.

— STEPHEN A. DOUGLAS,
*first debate with Abraham Lincoln,*
*Ottawa, Illinois, August 21, 1858*

*I will say here, while upon this subject,* that I have no purpose, directly or indirectly, to interfere with the institution of slavery in the States where it exists. I believe I have no lawful right to do so, and I have no inclination to do so. I have no purpose to introduce political and social equality between the white and the black races . . . but I hold that, notwithstanding all this, there is no reason in the world why the negro is not entitled to all the natural rights enumerated in the Declaration of Independence, the right to life, liberty, and the pursuit of happiness. I hold that he is as much entitled to these as the white man. I agree with Judge Douglas he is not my equal in many respects—certainly not in color, perhaps not in moral or intellectual endowment. But in the right to eat the bread, without the leave of anybody else, which his own hand earns, *he is my equal and the equal of Judge Douglas, and the equal of every living man.*

—Abraham Lincoln,
*reply to Stephen Douglas, first debate,*
*Ottawa, Illinois, August 21, 1858*

THOUGH THE DEFENSE of African slavery (thus it is commonly called) is left to the South, the North are jointly benefited by it. Deduct from their trade and manufacturers all which is dependent upon the products of slave labor, their prosperity would fade.

—U.S. SENATOR JEFFERSON DAVIS,
*speech to the Mississippi Democratic Convention,*
*July 6, 1859*

*This is a world of compensations; and he who would be no slave must consent to have no slave. Those who deny freedom to others deserve it not for themselves; and, under a just God, cannot long retain it.*

—ABRAHAM LINCOLN,
*letter to H. L. Pierce, April 6, 1859*

# THE APATHY OF THE PEOPLE

is enough to make every statue leap from its pedestal and hasten the resurrection of the dead.

—WILLIAM LLOYD GARRISON

I believe we have no power, under the Constitution of the United States; or rather under the form of government under which we live, to interfere with the institution of Slavery, or any other of the institutions of our sister States, *be they Free or Slave States.*

—ABRAHAM LINCOLN,
*speech in Cincinnati, Ohio,*
*September 17, 1859*

# I believe that to interfere, as I have done, in the behalf of God's despised poor is not wrong but right.

*Now, if it is deemed necessary that I should forfeit my life for the furtherance of the ends of justice, and mingle my blood further with the blood of my children and with the blood of millions in this slave country whose rights are disregarded by wicked, cruel, and unjust enactments,*

## I say, let it be done.

—John Brown,
court statement following being sentenced to death,
November 1, 1859

He is not Old Brown any longer;
## HE IS AN ANGEL OF LIGHT.

—HENRY DAVID THOREAU,
*A Plea for Captain John Brown*, 1859

*There is not a respectable system of civilization known to history whose foundations were not laid in the institution of domestic slavery.*

—ROBERT M. T. HUNTER,
*Senator from Virginia, quoted from* Battle Cry of Freedom, *James M. McPherson, 1988*

*There's two things I've got a right to . . .*
## DEATH OR LIBERTY.

—HARRIET TUBMAN,
*former slave, quoted by Sarah H. Bradford,*
Harriet Tubman, the Moses of Her People, *1886*

ALTHOUGH VOLUME
upon volume is written to prove slavery a very good
thing, we never hear of the man who wishes to take
the good of it, by being a slave himself.

—ABRAHAM LINCOLN

THE DIFFERENCE BETWEEN US IS, THAT OUR slaves are hired for life and well compensated; there is no starvation, no begging, no want of employment among our people, and not too much employment either. . . . We do not think that whites should be slaves either by law or necessity. Our slaves are black, of another and inferior race. The status in which we have placed them is an elevation. They are elevated from the condition in which God first created them, by being made our slaves.

—JAMES HENRY HAMMOND,
*speech before the United States Senate, March 4, 1858*

*Never chase a lie. Let it alone, and it will run itself to death.*

—LYMAN BEECHER

⚊

AFRICAN SLAVERY is the corner stone of the industrial, social, and political fabric of the South; and whatever wars against it, wars against her very existence. Strike down the institution of African slavery and you reduce the South to depopulation and barbarism.

— LAWRENCE KEITT,
*Congressman from South Carolina,*
*speech to the House on January 25, 1860*

MANY GOVERNMENTS HAVE BEEN FOUNDED upon the principle of the subordination and serfdom of certain classes of the same race; such were and are in violation of the laws of nature. Our system commits no such violation of nature's laws. With us, all of the white race, however high or low, rich or poor, are equal in the eye of the law. Not so with the Negro. Subordination is his place. He, by nature, or by the curse against Canaan, is fitted for that condition which he occupies in our system.

—C.S. VICE PRESIDENT ALEXANDER H. STEPHENS,
*speech in Savannah, Georgia, March 21, 1861,*
*quoted from the* Savannah Republican

*The traitor against the general government forfeits his slave, at least as justly as he does any other property;* and he forfeits both to the government against which he offends. The government, so far as there can be ownership, thus owns the forfeited slaves; and the question for Congress, in regard to them is, "Shall they be made free, or be sold to new masters?" I perceive no objection to Congress deciding in advance that they shall be free.

—ABRAHAM LINCOLN,
*message to the Congress, July 17, 1862*

*Emancipation is the demand of civilization. That is a principle; everything else is an intrigue.*

—Ralph Waldo Emerson, 1862

THE TRIUMPHS of Christianity rest this very hour upon slavery; and slavery depends on the triumphs of the South . . . This war is the servant of slavery.

—REVEREND JOHN T. WIGHTMAN,
*preaching at Yorkville, South Carolina,*
*The Glory of God, the Defence of the South, 1861,*
*cited in Eugene Genovese's* Consuming Fire, *1998*

WE ARE AMERICANS, SPEAKING THE SAME language, adopting the same customs, holding the same general opinions . . . and shall rise and fall with Americans.

—FREDERICK DOUGLASS

# IN GIVING FREEDOM TO THE SLAVE, WE ASSURE FREEDOM TO THE FREE.

*Honorable alike in what we give and what we preserve.*
*We shall nobly save, or meanly lose, the last, best hope of earth.*

—President Abraham Lincoln,
second annual message to Congress,
December 1, 1862

*Without slavery, the rebellion could never have existed. Without slavery, it could not continue.*

—Abraham Lincoln,
*message to Congress, December 1, 1862*

LOOKING UPON AFRICAN SLAVERY FROM THE same standpoint held by the noble framers of our Constitution, I have ever considered it one of the greatest blessings (for both themselves and us) that God ever bestowed upon a favorite nation.

—JOHN WILKES BOOTH,
*letter to his sister Asia, April 14, 1865*

*I am obliged to confess that I do not regard the abolition of slavery as a means of warding off the struggle of the two races in the Southern states.* The Negroes may long remain slaves without complaining; but if they are once raised to the level of freemen, they will soon revolt at being deprived of almost all their civil rights; and as they cannot become the equals of the whites, they will speedily show themselves as enemies.

—ALEXIS DE TOCQUEVILLE

*O*ne eighth of the whole population were col-ored slaves, not distributed generally over the Union, but localized in the Southern part of it. These slaves constituted a peculiar and powerful interest. All knew that this interest was, somehow, the cause of the war.

—Abraham Lincoln,
Inaugural Address, March 4, 1865

THE BLUNTING EFFECTS of slavery upon the slaveholder's moral percep-tions are known and conceded the world over; and a privileged class, an aristocracy, is but a band of slaveholders under another name.

—Mark Twain,
*A Connecticut Yankee in King Arthur's Court, 1889*

# THREE

# Terrible
# Swift Sword: 1861

I DO NOT KNOW
what the Union would be worth if saved by the use
of the sword.

—U.S. SENATOR FROM NEW YORK AND
SECRETARY OF STATE WILLIAM H. SEWARD,
*speech to the Senate, January 12, 1861*

*I shall await the first shot,*
*and if you do not batter us to pieces,*
*we shall be starved out in a few days.*

—U.S. MAJOR ROBERT ANDERSON,
ON DEPARTING FOR FORT SUMTER, APRIL 11, 1861

THE FIRING ON THAT FORT WILL INAUGURATE a civil war greater than any the world has yet seen ... you will lose us every friend at the North. You will wantonly strike a hornet's nest which extends from mountains to ocean. Legions now quiet will swarm out and sting us to death. It is unnecessary. It puts us in the wrong. It is fatal.

—C.S. SECRETARY OF STATE ROBERT TOOMBS,
*advice to Jefferson Davis prior to the attack on Fort Sumter,*
*April 13, 1861*

I sprang out of bed ... and on my knees—prostrate—
*I prayed as I never prayed before.*

—MARY CHESTNUT,
*diary entry on hearing the first bombardment*
*of Fort Sumter, April 13, 1861*

*Our Southern brethren have done grievously, they have rebelled and have attacked their father's house and their loyal brothers. They must be punished and brought back, but this necessity breaks my heart.*

—U.S. MAJOR ROBERT ANDERSON,
*comment after the evacuation of Fort Sumter,*
*April 14, 1861*

WHAT A CHANGE NOW GREETS US! The Government is aroused, the dead North is alive, and its divided people united . . . The cry now is for war, vigorous war, war to the bitter end, and war till the traitors are effectually and permanently put down.

—FREDERICK DOUGLASS,
*comment on the opening of hostilities after Fort Sumter,*
*May 1861*

# THEY DO NOT KNOW WHAT THEY SAY.

*If it came to a conflict of arms, the war will last at least four years. Northern politicians will not appreciate the determination and pluck of the South, and Southern politicians do not appreciate the numbers, resources, and patient perseverance of the North. Both sides forget that we are all Americans.*

*I foresee that our country will pass through a terrible ordeal, a necessary expiation, perhaps, for our national sins.*

—C.S. GENERAL ROBERT E. LEE,
MAY 5, 1861

# OURS IS A JUST WAR,

a holy cause. The invader must meet the fate he deserves and we must meet him as becomes us, as becomes men.

—C.S. MAJOR JOHN PELHAM

*For my own part, I consider the first necessity that is upon us, is proving that popular government is not an absurdity. We must settle this question now—whether in a free government the minority have the right to break it up whenever they choose. If we fail, it will go far to prove the incapability of the people to govern themselves.*

—PRESIDENT ABRAHAM LINCOLN,
*comment to secretary John Hay, May 1861, quoted by
Carl Sandburg in* Abraham Lincoln: The War Years, *1939*

# This is essentially a people's contest.

*On the side of the Union it is a struggle for maintaining in the world that a form and substance of government whose leading objective is to elevate the condition of men; to lift artificial weights from all shoulders; to clear the paths of laudable pursuit for all; to afford all an unfettered start at a*

## fair chance in the race of life.

—President Abraham Lincoln,
message to the special session of Congress, July 4, 1861

*Every man must be for the United States or against it.* There can be no neutrals in this war, only patriots—or traitors.

—Senator Stephen Douglas, 1861

## SARAH . . .

If the dead can come back to this earth and flit unseen around those they loved, I shall always be near you; in the gladdest days and in the darkest nights ... always, always. And if there be a soft breeze upon your cheek, it shall be my breath, and as the cool air fans your throbbing temple, it shall be my spirit passing by. Sarah, do not mourn me dead; think I am gone and wait for me, for we shall meet again.

—U.S. MAJOR SULLIVAN BALLOU,
*letter to his wife shortly before being killed*
*at First Bull Run, July 1861*

THE SOLDIER'S FIRST BATTLEFIELD IS MARKED by a variety of sensations; trembling fear, curiosity, and an insane desire to get up and leave, half-feeling of awe, a strange nervousness, doubt as to his fate, all mingle together, making his heart beat fast and his pulse thrill with nameless horror; his breathing becomes thick and his face deadly pale; no matter what may be the temperament of the man, the first battle causes him more agony of mind than all the other conflicts combined.

—C.S. PRIVATE ALEXANDER HUNTER,
*Johnny Reb and Billy Yank,* 1905

I TELL YOU, SIR, women would make a grand brigade—if it was not for snakes and spiders! They don't mind bullets—women are not afraid of bullets; but one big black snake would put a whole army to flight.

—C.S. LIEUTENANT GENERAL RICHARD S. EWELL,
*comment to Major John B. Gordon*
*prior to the Battle of First Manassas, July 21, 1861,*
Reminiscences of the Civil War, *John B Gordon, 1903*

———

*The enemy has assailed my outposts in heavy force. I have fallen back on the line of Bull Run and will make a stand at Mitchell's Ford.*

—C.S. GENERAL P.G.T. BEAUREGARD,
*telegram, July 17, 1861*

*Then, Sir, we will give them the bayonet!*

—C.S. LIEUTENANT GENERAL THOMAS J. JACKSON,
REPLY TO COLONEL B. E. BEE WHEN HE REPORTED
THAT THE ENEMY WERE FORCING THEM TO FALL BACK
AT THE FIRST BATTLE OF BULL RUN, JULY 17, 1861

LET US DETERMINE TO DIE HERE, AND WE
will conquer. There is Jackson standing like a stone wall!
Rally behind the Virginians!

—C.S. BRIGADIER GENERAL ELLIOT GERNARD BEE,
*first battle of Bull Run, July 21, 1861*

*The words, gestures, and threats of our officers were thrown away upon men who had lost all presence of mind and only longed for absence of body.*

—U.S. Colonel Andrew Potter,
*on the Union route at Bull Run, July 21, 1861*

It's bad. It's damned bad.

—Abraham Lincoln,
*first reaction to the Union Army's rout at First Bull Run, July 21, 1861*

## LITTLE DID I CONCEIVE

of the greatness of the defeat, the magnitude of the disaster which it had entailed upon the United States. So short-lived has been the American Union, that men who saw it rise may live to see it fall.

—WILLIAM HOWARD RUSSELL, *Times* (London), *reporting on the Union defeat at Bull Run, July 21, 1861*

## IT IS NOT CHARACTERISTIC OF AMERICANS

to sit down despondently after a defeat ... Reverses, though stunning at first, by their recoil stimulate and quicken to unwonted exertion ... Let us go to work, then, with a will.

—*New York Tribune*, JULY 30, 1861

# CAPTAIN, MY RELIGIOUS BELIEF TEACHES ME TO FEEL AS SAFE IN BATTLE AS IN BED.

*God has fixed the time for my death. I do not concern myself about that, but to be always ready, no matter when it may overtake me. That is the way all men should live,*

*and then all would be equally brave.*

—C.S. LT. GENERAL THOMAS J. JACKSON,
ANSWER TO CAPTAIN JOHN D. IMBODEN'S QUESTION
AS TO THE SOURCE OF JACKSON'S CALMNESS UNDER FIRE,
*Stonewall Jackson and the American Civil War,*
G.F.R HENDERSON, VOL. I

*A private soldier is but an automaton*, a machine that works by the command of a good, bad, or indifferent engineer, and is presumed to know nothing of all these great events. His business is to load and shoot, stand picket, videt, etc., while the officers sleep, or perhaps die on the field of battle and glory, and his obituary and epitaph but "one" remembered among the slain, but to what company, regiment, brigade or corps he belongs, there is no account; *he is soon forgotten.*

—C.S. PRIVATE SAM WATKINS,
*"Co. Aytch": A Side Show of the Big Show,* 1881

*This is not an army. It will take a long time to make an army.*

—U.S. Brigadier General Irvin McDowell, July 1861,
quoted by Nathaniel W. Stephenson in
*Lincoln: An Account of His Personal Life,* 1922

*We may be annihilated, but we cannot be conquered.*

—C.S. GENERAL ALBERT SIDNEY JOHNSTON, CSA,
IN ACCEPTING HIS COMMAND RANK, AUGUST 1861

THE FIRST THING
in the morning is drill, then drill, then drill again.
Then drill, drill, a little more drill. Then drill, and
lastly drill. Between drills we drill and sometimes
stop to eat a little and have a roll call.

—U.S. PRIVATE OLIVER W. NORTON,
*letter to a friend, October 9, 1861, quoted from*
Soldiers Blue and Gray, *James I. Robertson, 1998*

It's just like shooting squirrels, only these squirrels
have guns.

—A FEDERAL VETERAN INSTRUCTING
NEW RECRUITS AT WEAPONS TRAINING

*T*he contest is really for empire on the side of
the North and for independence on that of the
South.

—*Times* (LONDON), NOVEMBER 7, 1861

A THOUGHTFUL MIND, WHEN IT SEES A nation's flag, sees not a flag only, but the nation itself; and whatever may be its symbols, its insignia, be read chiefly in the flag of the government, the principles, the truths, the history which belongs to the nation that sets it forth.

—HENRY WARD BEECHER, *"The National Flag," 1861*

*The Mississippi is the backbone of the Rebellion;* it is the key to the whole situation. While the confederates hold it they can obtain supplies of all kinds, and it is a barrier against our forces.

—PRESIDENT ABRAHAM LINCOLN,
*comment to Commander David D. Porter,*
*November 12, 1861, quoted from*
Battles and Leaders of the Civil War, *vol. 2, 1888*

*Sickness is more to be dreaded by far in the army, than the bullets. No bravery can achieve any thing against it. The soldier may sicken and die, without receiving any attention but from the rough hands of his fellow soldiers. When buried he is as soon forgotten. Not a stone is raised to tell his living name, age or face. But many a bitter tear is shed over his melancholy fate by kind friends far away.*

—C.S. CORPORAL JAMES E. HALL,
*diary entry, November 19, 1861,*
The Diary of a Confederate Soldier, *1961*

# I have been a Soldier

all my life—I was an officer in the Army of the U.S., which service I left to fight for my own country, and for, and with, my own People—and because they were right, and oppressed.

—C.S. Brigadier General Lewis A. Armistead,
*letter to Samuel Cooper, December 21, 1861*

*I don't know how long it has been* since my ear has been free from the roll of a drum. It is the music I sleep by, and I love it. . . . I shall remain here while anyone remains, and do whatever comes to my hand. I may be compelled to face danger, but never fear it, and while our soldiers can stand and fight, I can stand and feed and nurse them.

—Clara Barton, letter to her father, 1861

# So the case stands, and under all the passion of the parties and the cries of battle lie the two chief moving causes of the struggle.

*Union means so many millions a year lost to the South; secession means the loss of the same millions to the North. The love of money is the root of this, as of many other evils. The quarrel between the North and South is, as it stands,*

## *solely a fiscal quarrel.*

—CHARLES DICKENS,
"ALL THE YEAR ROUND,"
DECEMBER 28, 1861

*The war between the North and the South is a tariff war. The war is further, not for any principle, does not touch the question of slavery, and in fact turns on the Northern lust for sovereignty.*

—KARL MARX, 1861

FOUR

# Mr. Lincoln's
# *War: 1862*

*Mine eyes have seen the glory of the coming of the Lord;*
*He is trampling out the vintage where the grapes of wrath*
*are stored; He hath loosed the fateful lightning of his*
*terrible swift sword: His truth is marching on.*

—Julia Ward Howe,
*Battle Hymn of the Republic,* 1862

No terms except unconditional surrender can be accepted. I propose to move immediately upon your works.

—U.S. General Ulysses S. Grant,
*message to C.S. Brigadier General Simon Bolivar Buckner,*
*Fort Donelson, Tennessee, February 16, 1862*

*Boys, these people are talking about surrendering, and I am going out of this place before they do or bust hell wide open!*

—C.S. Lieutenant Colonel Nathan Bedford Forrest,
*oath to his men before escaping from the siege at*
*Fort Donelson, Tennessee, February 16, 1862*

. . . a tyrannical, hot-headed VULGARIAN.

—as subordinate's description of
Nathan Bedford Forrest

**A MILLION MEN, IT IS ESTIMATED, ARE NOW STANDING IN HOSTILE ARRAY AND WAGING WAR ALONG A FRONTIER OF THOUSANDS OF MILES.**

*Battles have been fought, sieges have been conducted, and although the contest is not ended and the tide for the moment is against us, the final result in our favor is not doubtful. We have had our trials and difficulties. That we are to escape them in the future is not to be hoped. It was to be expected when we entered this war that it would expose our people to sacrifices and cost them much, both of money and blood. But the picture has its lights as well as its shadows.*

*This great strife has awakened in the people the highest emotions and qualities of the human soul.*

—JEFFERSON DAVIS,
SECOND INAUGURAL ADDRESS, FEBRUARY 22, 1862

# WE CONTINUED TO FIRE

at the *Minnesota*, and blew up a steamer alongside of her, and we also engaged the *Monitor*, sometimes at very close quarters. We once succeeded in running into her, and twice silenced her fire. The pilots declaring that we could get no nearer the *Minnesota*, and believing her to be entirely disabled, and the *Monitor* having to run into shoal water, which prevented our doing her any further injury, we ceased firing at twelve and proceeded to Norfolk. Our loss is 2 killed and 19 wounded.

—C.S. LIEUTENANT JONES,
*reporting of the action between the USS* Monitor *and the CSS* Virginia *on March 9, 1862*

AFTER A STORMY PASSAGE, WHICH PROVED us to be the finest seaboat I was ever in, we fought the *Merrimack* for more than three hours this forenoon and sent her back to Norfolk in a sinking condition. Ironclad against ironclad. We maneuvered about the bay here and went at each other with mutual fierceness. I consider that both ships were well fought. We were struck 22 times— pilot house twice, turret 9 times, side armor 8 times, deck 3 times. The only vulnerable point was the pilot house.... She tried to run us down and sink us, as she did the *Cumberland* yesterday, but she got the worst of it.

—U.S. CHIEF ENGINEER STIMERS, USS *Monitor*,
*reporting of the action between the USS* Monitor *and the
CSS* Virginia *on March 9, 1862.*

\* The USS *Merrimack* was the original name of the ship before
Confederate engineers converted it to the ironclad CSS *Virginia*.

*As gunpowder made armor useless on shore, so armor is having its revenge by baffling its old enemy at sea; and that, while gunpowder robbed land warfare of nearly all its picturesqueness to give even greater stateliness and sublimity to a sea-fight, armor bids fare to degrade the latter into a squabble between two iron-shelled turtles.*

—James Russell Lowell,
*comment on the first clash of ironclads on March 9, 1862, between the USS* Monitor *and the CSS* Virginia

*Our affairs look dark, but not hopeless.* The war may be a long one, but it *can* have but one termination—our independence. We are stimulated to new exertion, our people are roused to action, and there exists a deep-seated resolve in the heart of the nation, *to choose extermination before subjugation.*

—C.S. LIEUTENANT RANDOLPH H. McKIM,
*letter to his mother, March 10, 1862*

I AM TO WATCH OVER YOU as a parent over his own children; and you know that your general loves you from the depths of his heart.

—U.S. MAJOR GENERAL GEORGE B. McCLELLAN,
*speech to his troops, March 1862*

I FEEL TO THANK GOD THAT HE HAS KEPT me within his fold while so many have gone astray, and trust that he will give me Grace to continue to serve Him and my country faithfully. I have now been in service ten months and feel like a veteran. Sleeping on the ground is fun, and a bed of pine boughs better than one of feathers.

—U.S. PRIVATE ELISHA HUNT RHODES, MARCH 21, 1862, *All for the Union: The Civil War Diary & Letters of Elisha Hunt Rhodes*, 1991

*Lee's strategy was indeed remarkable. He knew McClellan and he knew Lincoln. He knew that the former was over-cautious; he knew that the latter was over-anxious.*

—BRITISH LIEUTENANT COLONEL G.F.R. HENDERSON, *Stonewall Jackson and the American Civil War*, vol. 1, 1898

*We always understood each other so well.* I fear they may continue to make these changes till they find someone whom I don't understand.

—C.S. General Robert E. Lee,
*comment on the replacement of*
*Union General George B. McClellan*

He has got the slows, Mr. Blair.

—Abraham Lincoln,
*comment to Francis Blair concerning*
*General McClellan's removal from command*

*W*hen a fellow's time comes, down he goes. Every bullet has its billet.

—C.S. PRIVATE EDMUND D. PATTERSON,
*diary entry, April 4, 1862, quoted by Bell Irvin Wiley in*
Life of Johnny Reb, *1943*

TONIGHT we water our horses in the Tennessee River.

—C.S. GENERAL ALBERT SIDNEY JOHNSTON,
*comment before attacking Union forces at*
*Shiloh, Tennessee, April 6, 1862*

AT FOUR O'CLOCK in the morning we began the march on the enemy. Each man had forty cartridges, all moving accoutrements and three days' rations. General Johnston was cheered as he rode by our command and I remember his words as well as if they had been today, "Shoot low, boys; it takes two to carry one off the field."

—C.S. PRIVATE WILLIAM E. BEVENS, *on the advance at Shiloh, Tennessee, on the morning of April 6, 1862,* Reminiscences of a Private, *Daniel E. Sutherland (ed.) 1992*

*The rebels are out there thicker than fleas on a dog's back!*

—A UNION OFFICER REPORTING THE ADVANCE OF CONFEDERATE FORCES AT SHILOH, TENNESSEE, APRIL 6, 1862

*Retreat?*
NO. I propose to attach at daylight and whip them.

—U.S. Major General Ulysses S. Grant,
*to Colonel James B. McPherson, Shiloh,*
*evening of April 6, 1862*

The blue and the gray were mingled
together . . . It was no uncommon thing to see the bodies of
Federal and Confederate lying side by side as though they
had bled to death while trying to aid each other.

—U.S. Private John A. Cockerill,
*recalling the aftermath of the battle at Shiloh*

# The horrible sights that I have witnessed on this field I can never describe.

*No blaze of glory, that flashes around the magnificent triumphs of war, can ever atone for the unwritten and unutterable* *horrors of the scene.*

—U.S. Brigadier General James A. Garfield, letter to his wife, April 1862

Skimming lightly, wheeling still,
    The swallows fly low
Over the field in clouded days,
    The forest-field of Shiloh —
Over the field where April rain
Solaced the parched ones stretched in pain
Through the pause of night
That followed the Sunday fight
    Around the church of Shiloh —
The church so lone, the log-built one,
That echoed so many a parting groan
    And natural prayer
    Of dying foemen mingled there —
Foemen at morn, but friends at eve —
    Fame or country least their care:
(What like a bullet can undeceive!)
    But now they lie low,
While over them the swallows skim
    And all is hushed at Shiloh.

—Herman Melville,
*"Shiloh: A Requiem"*

*I'm fighting because you are down here.*

—CONFEDERATE PRISONER,
WHEN ASKED WHY HE WAS FIGHTING IN THE WAR
BY A UNION SOLDIER, SHILOH, APRIL 1862

I can't spare this man—HE FIGHTS!

—ABRAHAM LINCOLN,
*comment to friend Colonel A. K. McClure in defense of*
*Ulysses S. Grant following the battle of Shiloh, 1862,*
*quoted from* Lincoln's Yarns and Stories, *A. K. McClure*

*The dead of the battlefield come up to us very rarely, even in dreams. We see the list in the morning paper at breakfast, but dismiss its recollection with the coffee. Mr. Matthew Brady has done something to bring us the terrible reality and earnestness of the war. If he has not brought bodies and laid them in our door-yards and along our streets, he has done something very like it.*

—*New York Times,*
EDITORIAL ON THE PHOTOGRAPHY OF
MATTHEW B. BRADY, 1862

# AT PRECISELY TWENTY MINUTES OF FOUR O'CLOCK THE ENEMY OPENED FIRE FROM FORT ST. PHILIP ...

*Shot, shell, grape, and canister filled the air with deadly missiles. It was like the breaking up of a thousand worlds—crash—tear—whiz! Such another scene was never witnessed by mortal man. Steadily we steamed on, giving them shell, the forts firing rifle-shot and shell, 10-inch Columbiads, 42, 32, and 24 pounder balls; and, to add to this state of affairs, 13 steamers and the floating battery Louisiana, of the enemy, were pouring into and around us a hail-storm of iron perfectly indescribable.*

*Not satisfied with their firing, fire-raft after fire-raft was lit and set adrift to do their work of burning.*

—*Harper's Weekly*,
EYEWITNESS ACCOUNT OF UNION SHIPS UNDER
ADMIRAL FARRAGUT RUNNING UP THE MISSISSIPPI
TO CAPTURE NEW ORLEANS, APRIL 16, 1862

WAR SEEMS A GAME OF CHESS, but we have an unequal number of pawns to begin with. We have knights, kings, queens, bishops, and castles enough. But our skillful generals, whenever they cannot arrange the board to suit them exactly, burn everything and march away.

—MARY BOYKIN CHESTNUT,
*wife of South Carolina senator James Chestnut Jr., diary entry, April 29, 1862,* A Diary from Dixie, *1905*

Don't flinch boys! They're shooting at me, not at you!

—U.S. BRIGADIER GENERAL PHILIP KEARNY,
*Williamsburg, Virginia, May 5, 1862*

*I don't believe in Secession, but I do in Liberty.* I want the South to conquer, dictate its own terms, and go back to the Union, for I believe that, apart, inevitable ruin awaits both. It is a rope of sand, this Confederacy, founded on the doctrine of Secession, and will not last many years—not five. The North cannot subdue us. We are too determined to be free. They have no right to confiscate our property to pay debts they themselves have incurred. Death as a nation, rather than Union on such terms. We will have our rights secured on so firm a basis that it can never be shaken. If by power of overwhelming numbers they conquer us, *it will be a barren victory over a desolate land.*

—Sarah Morgan Dawson,
*A Confederate Girl's Diary,*
ed. James I. Robertson, 1960

*Before this war is over, I intend to be a major general or a corpse.*

—C.S. BRIGADIER GENERAL ISAAC R. TRIMBLE,
*letter to daughter*

PEOPLE HERE ARE QUITE STRUCK ABACK at Sunday's news of the capture of New Orleans. It took them three days to make up their minds to believe it. The division of American had become an idea so fixed that they had about shut out all the avenues to the reception of any other.

—HENRY BROOKS ADAMS,
*writing from London*

AS THE OFFICERS and Soldiers of the United States have been subject to repeated insults from the women calling themselves ladies of New Orleans, in return for the most scrupulous non-interference and courtesy on our part, it is ordered that hereafter when any Female shall, by word, gesture, or movement, insult or show contempt for any officer of the United States, she shall be regarded and held liable to be treated as a woman of the town plying her avocation.

—U.S. MAJOR GENERAL BENJAMIN BUTLER,
*military governor New Orleans*
*General Orders No. 28, May 15, 1862*

*Butler is branded a felon, an outlaw, an enemy of Mankind,* and so ordered that in the event of his capture, the officer in command of the capturing force do cause him to be immediately executed by hanging.

—JEFFERSON DAVIS ON HEARING OF BUTLER'S GENERAL ORDER AGAINST THE WOMEN OF NEW ORLEANS

*I was always a friend of southern rights,*
*but an enemy of southern wrongs.*

— U.S. MAJOR GENERAL BENJAMIN BUTLER,
UNION MILITARY GOVERNOR, NEW ORLEANS

I don't fear McClellan or anyone in Yankeedom.

—C.S. Major General James Longstreet,
*letter to C.S. Major General Gustavus W. Smith,*
*June 1, 1862*

---

# If I save this Army now

I tell you plainly that I owe no thanks to you or any other persons in Washington—you have done your best to sacrifice this Army.

—U.S. Major General George B. McClellan,
*telegram to Abraham Lincoln*
*during the Seven Days Battles, June 1862*

*The only true rule for cavalry is to follow the enemy as long as he retreats.*

—C.S. Lieutenant General Jackson to Colonel Munford on June 13, 1862, G. F. R. Henderson, *Stonewall Jackson and the American Civil War*, 1995

*I had rather be a private in such an Army than a Field Officer in any other Army.*

—A Confederate soldier's view on General "Stonewall" Jackson's Shenandoah Valley campaign, June 1862

OVER FIVE THOUSAND DEAD AND WOUNDED men were on the ground in every attitude of distress. A third of them were dead or dying, but enough were alive and moving to give to the field a singular crawling effect.

—U.S. MAJOR GENERAL WILLIAM W. AVERELL, *describing the morning after the battle of Malvern Hill, Virginia, on July 1, 1862. Quoted from* The Battle Cry of Freedom: The Civil War *by James M. McPherson 1989*

*We must free the slaves or be ourselves subdued. The slaves were undeniably an element of strength to those who had their service, and we must decide whether that element should be with us or against us.*

—PRESIDENT ABRAHAM LINCOLN, *comment to Secretary of the Navy Gideon Welles, July 13, 1862, quoted from James M. McPherson,* The Battle Cry of Freedom, *1989*

# I HAVE COME TO YOU FROM THE WEST, WHERE WE HAVE ALWAYS SEEN THE BACKS OF OUR ENEMIES;

*from an army whose business it has been to seek the adversary and to beat him when he was found; whose policy has been attack and not defense. In but one instance has the enemy been able to place our Western armies in defensive attitude. I presume that I have been called here to pursue the same system and to lead you against the enemy.*

*It is my purpose to do so, and that speedily.*

—U.S. Major General John Pope,
message to the Army of Virginia, July 14, 1862

*Headquarters in the Saddle*

—U.S. MAJOR GENERAL JOHN POPE,
SIGNATURE TO MESSAGES

I DEPLORE THE WAR as much as ever, but if the thing has to be done, let the means be adequate. Don't expect to overrun such a country or subdue such a people in two or five years. It is the task of a century.

—U.S. BRIGADIER GENERAL
WILLIAM TECUMSEH SHERMAN,
*letter to his brother, U.S. senator John Sherman of Ohio,*
*August 13, 1862*

I can whip any man who does not know
his headquarters from his hindquarters.

—C.S. LIEUTENANT GENERAL THOMAS J. JACKSON,
ATTRIBUTED

*We cannot conquer ten millions of people
united in solid phalanx against us, pow-
erfully aided by Northern sympathizers and Euro-
pean allies. We must have scouts, guides, spies, cooks,
teamsters, diggers, and choppers from the blacks of the
South, whether we allow them to fight for us or not,
or we shall be baffled and repelled.*

—HORACE GREELEY, EDITORIAL,
*New York Tribune,* August 19, 1862

THE GOVERNMENT SEEMS DETERMINED TO apply the guillotine to all unsuccessful generals. It seems rather hard to do this where the general is not in fault, but perhaps with us now, as in the French Revolution, some harsh measures are required.

—U.S. MAJOR GENERAL HENRY W. HALLECK,
*letter to Major General Horatio Wright, August 25, 1862*

*Boys, he isn't much for looks,* but if we'd had him we wouldn't have been caught in this trap.

—FEDERAL PRISONER OF WAR TO HIS FELLOW CAPTIVES
AT HARPERS FERRY IN REFERENCE TO
STONEWALL JACKSON, SEPTEMBER 1862

# Always mystify, mislead and surprise the enemy, if possible.

*And when you strike and overcome him, never let up in the pursuit so long as your men have strength to follow. The other rule is, never fight against heavy odds if by any possible maneuvering you can hurl your own force on only a part, and that the weakest part, of your enemy and crush it. Such tactics will win every time, and a small army may thus destroy a large one in detail,* and repeated victory will make it invincible.

—C.S. Lieutenant General Thomas J. Jackson

*T*he Kentuckians are slow and backward in rallying to our standard. Their hearts are evidently with us, but their blue-grass and fat cattle are against us.

—C.S. MAJOR GENERAL EDMUND KIRBY SMITH,
*letter to General Braxton Bragg, September 1862*

"JEB" STUART
is my ideal of a cavalry leader; prompt, vigilant, and fearless.

—C.S. LIEUTENANT GENERAL THOMAS J. JACKSON,
*quoted by C.S. Major General Daniel H. Hill*
*in* Century Magazine, *February 1894*

*I never see one of Jackson's couriers approach* without expecting an order to assault the North Pole.

—C.S. MAJOR GENERAL RICHARD EWELL

IN A SECOND THE AIR WAS FULL OF THE hiss of bullets and the hurtle of grapeshot. The mental strain was so great that I saw at that moment the singular effect mentioned, I think in the life of Goethe on a similar occasion—the whole landscape for an instant turned slightly red.

—U.S. PRIVATE DAVID L. THOMPSON,
*describing the battle of Antietam, Maryland,*
*September 17, 1862, quoted in*
Battles and Leaders of the Civil War, *vol. 2, 1888*

*The day had been a long one, but the evening seemed longer; the sun seemed almost to go backwards, and it appeared as if night would never come.*

—C.S. Lieutenant James A. Graham,
*27th North Carolina Infantry, Antietam, Maryland, September 17, 1862*

Every stalk of corn in the northern and greater part of the field was cut as closely as could have been done with a knife, and the slain lay in rows precisely as they stood in their ranks a few minutes before.

—a Union officer describing the aftermath of battle at Antietam, Maryland, September 17, 1862

WHEREAS ON THE 22ND DAY OF SEPTEMBER, A.D. 1862, A PROCLAMATION WAS ISSUED BY THE PRESIDENT OF THE UNITED STATES, CONTAINING, AMONG OTHER THINGS, THE FOLLOWING, TO WIT:

*That on the 1st day of January, A.D. 1863, all persons held as slaves within any State or designated part of a State the people whereof shall then be in rebellion against the United States shall be then, thenceforward, and forever free; and the executive government of the United States, including the military and naval authority thereof, will recognize and maintain the freedom of such persons and will do no act or acts to repress such persons, or any of them, in any efforts they may make for their actual freedom.*

—Abraham Lincoln,
September 22, 1862

*A restitution of the Union
has been rendered forever impossible.*

—JEFFERSON DAVIS IN REACTION
TO THE EMANCIPATION PROCLAMATION

WE MAY HAVE OUR OWN OPINIONS ABOUT
slavery, we may be for or against the South; but there is no
doubt that Jefferson Davis and other leaders of the South
have made an army; they are making, it appears, a navy;
and they have made, what is more than either—
they have made a nation.

—SIR WILLIAM GLADSTONE,
*Chancellor of the Exchequer,
speech at Newcastle, England, October 1862*

I HAVE JUST READ your dispatch about sore-tongued and fatigued horses, Will you pardon me for asking what the horses of your army have done since the Battle of Antietam that fatigues anything?

—ABRAHAM LINCOLN,
*telegram to General McClellan, October 25, 1862*

So you're the little woman who wrote
**the book that made this great war!**

—ABRAHAM LINCOLN,
*to Harriet Beecher Stowe at their first meeting
at the White House*

## Fellow-citizens,
### WE CANNOT ESCAPE HISTORY . . .

*In giving freedom to the slave, we assure freedom to the free—*
*honorable alike in what we give, and what we preserve.*
*We shall nobly save, or meanly lose, the last best hope of earth.*
*Other means may succeed; this could not fail.*

*The way is plain, peaceful, generous, just—*
*a way which, if followed, the world will forever*
*applaud, and God must forever bless.*

—Abraham Lincoln
MESSAGE TO CONGRESS, DECEMBER I, 1862

*O*h, I know where Lee's forces are, and I expect to surprise him, I expect to cross and occupy the hills before Lee can bring anything serious to meet me.

—U.S. MAJOR GENERAL BURNSIDE,
*comment before moving against Marye's Heights,*
*Fredericksburg, Virginia, December 1862*

*If you make the attack as contemplated* it will be the greatest slaughter of the war; there isn't infantry enough in our whole army to carry those Heights if they are well defended.

—U.S. COLONEL P. C. HAWKINS,
*9th New York, statement to General Burnside,*
*Fredericksburg, Virginia, December 1862*

# GENERAL,

we cover that ground now so well that we comb it as with a fine-tooth comb. A chicken could not live on that field when we open on it.

—C.S. Colonel E. P. Alexander,
*1st Corps Artillery Chief, comment to General Longstreet before the Union advance on Marye's Heights, Fredericksburg, Virginia, December 13, 1862*

*We lost color bearer after color bearer,* I picked up the colors three times myself. The flagstaff was shot off and the flag perforated in 19 places by Rebel bullets.

—U.S. Lieutenant D. R. Coders,
*11th Penn. Reserves, Fredericksburg, Virginia, December 13, 1862*

*Every man has a sprig of green in his cap and a half-laughing, half-murderous look in their eyes.*

—U.S. CAPTAIN THOMAS F. GALAWAY,
*on the advance of the Irish Brigade,*
*Fredericksburg, December 13, 1862*

—

What a pity. Here comes Meagher's fellows.

—A CONFEDERATE IRISHMAN,
*comment before firing point blank into the ranks of the Union*
*Irish Brigade, Fredericksburg, December 13, 1862*

—

*Come on blue belly!*
*Bring them boots and blankets! Bring'em hyar!*

—A CONFEDERATE PRIVATE,
FREDERICKSBURG, DECEMBER 13, 1862

IT IS GLORIOUS to see such courage in one so young.

—C.S. GENERAL ROBERT E. LEE,
*speaking of C.S. Major Pelham's action at Fredericksburg,
Virginia, December 13, 1862*

IT IS WELL THAT WAR
is so terrible. We should grow too fond of it.

—C.S. GENERAL ROBERT E. LEE,
*comment to General Longstreet, observing the battle at
Fredericksburg, Virginia, December 13, 1862*

BUT OUT OF THAT SILENCE ROSE NEW SOUNDS more appalling still; a strange ventriloquism, of which you could not locate the source, a smothered moan, as if a thousand discords were flowing together into a key-note weird, unearthly, terrible to hear and bear, yet startling with its nearness; the writhing concord broken by cries for help, some begging for a drop of water, some calling on God for pity; and some on friendly hands to finish what the enemy had so horribly begun; some with delirious, dreamy voices murmuring loved names, as if the dearest were bending over them; and underneath, all the time, the deep bass note from closed lips too hopeless, or too heroic, to articulate their agony.

—U.S. Lt. Colonel Joshua Lawrence Chamberlain, *20th Maine, describing the night of December 13, 1862, after the end of the first day's combat at Fredericksburg, Virginia,* "Bayonet! Forward": My Civil War Reminiscences

*If there is a worse place than Hell,* I am in it.

—ABRAHAM LINCOLN,
UPON HEARING OF THE UNION DISASTER
AT FREDERICKSBURG, DECEMBER 1862

IT CAN HARDLY BE
in human nature for men to show more valor, or
generals to manifest less judgment.

—ANONYMOUS NORTHERN REPORTER
AT FREDERICKSBURG, DECEMBER 1862

I KNOW OF NO BRAVER MEN IN EITHER army than the Union troops at Fredericksburg, which was a serious Union defeat. But to keep charging that wall at the foot of Marye's Heights after all the failures there'd been is a singular instance of valor. It was different from southern élan. It was a steadiness under fire, a continuing to press the point.

—SHELBY FOOTE,
*The Civil War: An Illustrated History,*
Geoffrey C. Ward, Ric Burns, Ken Burns, 1990

*There they were, "our brave boys," as the papers justly called them, for cowards could hardly have been so riddled with shot and shell, so torn and shattered, nor have borne suffering for which we have no name, with an uncomplaining fortitude, which made one glad to cherish each other as a brother.*

—LOUISA MAY ALCOTT,
*letter describing the wounded from the
battle of Fredericksburg, December 1862,
later published in* Hospital Sketches, *1863*

---

*But what a cruel thing is war;* to separate and destroy families and friends, and mar the purest happiness God has granted us in this world; to fill our hearts with hatred instead of love for our neighbors, and to devastate the fair face of this beautiful world.

—C.S. LIEUTENANT GENERAL THOMAS J. JACKSON,
*letter to his wife, Mary Anna, December 25, 1862*

# THIS IS CHRISTMAS,

and my mind wanders back to that home made lonesome by my absence, while far away from the peace and quietude of civil life to undergo the hardships of the camp, and may be the battle field. I think of the many lives that are endangered, and hope that the time will soon come when peace, with its innumerable blessings, shall once more restore our country to happiness and prosperity.

—U.S. CORPORAL J. C. WILLIAMS,
*letter home, December 25, 1862*

---

*The Northern onslaught upon slavery was no more than a piece of specious humbug designed to conceal its desire for economic control of the Southern states.*

—CHARLES DICKENS, 1862

BE COOL—I NEED NOT ASK YOU TO BE BRAVE.
Keep ranks, do not throw away your fire; fire slowly, deliberately—above all, fire low, and be always sure of your aim.
Close readily in upon the enemy, and when you get within charging distance, rush upon him with the bayonet.
Do this and victory will certainly be yours.

—U.S. MAJOR GENERAL WILLIAM S. ROSECRANS,
*orders to his troops before the battle of Stone's River,*
*Murfreesboro, Tennessee, December 31, 1862*

# FIVE

# The High Watermark *of the* Confederacy: 1863

*That on the first day of January,* in the year of our Lord one thousand eight hundred and sixty-three, all persons held as slaves within any State or designated part of a State, the people whereof shall then be in rebellion against the United States, *shall be then, thenceforward, and forever free . . .*

—The Emancipation Proclamation, January 1, 1863

*As far as regards the action of this Government on such criminals as may attempt its execution, I confine myself to informing you that I shall, unless in your wisdom you deem some other course more expedient, deliver to the several State authorities all commissioned officers of the United States that may hereafter be captured by our forces in any of the States embraced in the proclamation, that they may be dealt with in accordance with the laws of those States, providing for the punishment of criminals engaged in exciting servile insurrections.*

—JEFFERSON DAVIS,
*"Jefferson Davis's Message,"*
Harper's Weekly, *January 31, 1863*

THE UNION GOVERNMENT liberates the enemy's slaves as it would the enemy's cattle, simply to weaken them in the conflict. The principle is not that a human being cannot justly own another, but that he cannot own him unless he is loyal to the United States.

—*London Spectator,*
ON THE EMANCIPATION PROCLAMATION,
JANUARYS 1863

*We are not fighting for slavery.* We are fighting for independence.

—JEFFERSON DAVIS

## THE FIRST OF JANUARY, 1863, WAS A MEMORABLE DAY IN THE PROGRESS OF AMERICAN LIBERTY AND CIVILIZATION.

*It was the turning-point in the conflict between freedom and slavery. A death blow was then given to the slaveholding rebellion. Until then the federal arm had been more than tolerant to that relict of barbarism. . . . We fought the rebellion, but not its cause. And now, on this day of January 1st, 1863, the formal and solemn announcement was made that thereafter the government would be found on the side of emancipation.*

*This proclamation changed everything.*

—FREDERICK DOUGLASS,
*Life and Times of Frederick Douglass,* 1881

IT WAS NO LONGER A QUESTION OF THE UNION as it was, that was to be re-established, but the Union as it should be. That is to say, washed clean from its original sin. We were no longer merely the soldiers of a political controversy, we were now missionaries on a great work of redemption, the armed liberators of millions. The war was ennobled. The object was higher.

—U.S. COLONEL REGIS DE TROBIAND, *after the Emancipation Proclamation, January 1863*

*With such noble women at home and such heroic soldiers in the field, we are invincible.*

—JEFFERSON DAVIS, *Richmond, Virginia, January 5, 1863*

*In saving the Union, I have destroyed the republic.*
Before me I have the Confederacy which I loath. But
behind me I have the bankers which I fear.

—ABRAHAM LINCOLN,
*comment on the National Bank Act, February 1863*

—

*I had rather lose one man in marching than five in fighting.*

—C.S. LIEUTENANT GENERAL THOMAS J. JACKSON,
quoted by Lieutenant Colonel G.F. R. Henderson in
*Stonewall Jackson and the American Civil War,* vol. 1, 1898

—

Conquer or be conquered.

—U.S. REAR ADMIRAL DAVID FARRAGUT

## IF WE OPPOSE FORCE

to force we cannot win, for their resources are greater than ours. We must substitute esprit for numbers. Therefore I strive to inculate in my men the spirit of the chase.

—C.S. MAJOR GENERAL J. E. B. STUART,
*quoted by Shelby Foote,* The Civil War, *vol. 1, 1958*

*If you won't go home,* return my visit
*and bring me a sack of coffee.*

—C.S. BRIGADIER GENERAL FITZHUGH LEE,
NOTE LEFT FOR HIS OLD FRIEND BRIGADIER GENERAL WIL-
LIAM W. AVERELL AFTER A CAVALRY RAID NEAR HARTWOOD
CHURCH, VIRGINIA, FEBRUARY 25, 1863

*Dear Fitz:*
Here's your coffee. Here's your visit. How did you like it?

—U.S. BRIGADIER GENERAL WILLIAM W. AVERELL,
*note left in reply to General Fitzhugh Lee following*
*the Battle of Kelly's Ford, Virginia, March 17, 1863*

*In my opinion the opening of the Mississippi River will be to us of more advantage than the capture of forty Richmonds.*

—U.S. MAJOR GENERAL HENRY W. HALLECK,
*telegram to Major General Ulysses S. Grant,*
*March 20, 1863*

THE COLORED POPULATION IS THE GREAT available and yet unavailed of force for restoring the Union. The bare sight of fifty thousand armed and drilled black soldiers upon the banks of the Mississippi would end the rebellion at once; and who doubts that we can present that sight if we but take hold in earnest?

—PRESIDENT ABRAHAM LINCOLN,
*letter to Andrew Johnson, March 26, 1863*

THIS WAR, DISGUISE IT as they may, is virtually nothing more or less than perpetual slavery against universal freedoms.

—*Frederick Douglass*

*Will the slave fight?* If any man asks you, tell him "no" ... But, if anyone asks you, will a Negro fight? Tell him YES!

—Abolitionist Wendell Phillips

*I wish to see the shackles struck from every slave.*

—C.S. Lieutenant General Thomas J. Jackson, attributed

*O*nly *those generals who gain success can set up dictators. What I ask of you is military success, and I will risk the dictatorship.*

—President Abraham Lincoln,
*letter to Brigadier General Joseph Hooker, appointing him to command the Army of the Potomac, January 26, 1863*

*My plans are perfect,* and when I start to carry them out, may God have mercy on Bobby Lee, for I shall have none.

—U.S. Major General Joseph Hooker,
April 12, 1863

## JACKSON USED NEITHER TOBACCO, NOR COFFEE, NOR SPIRITS;

*he would go all winter without cloak or overcoat in the mountains of Virginia, giving no other reason than that he "did not wish to give way to cold." These peculiarities were laughed at, and he was regarded as a marvel of eccentricity. But there was nothing erratic in it. This self-denial and self-control explain his wonderful success.*

*He had conquered himself, and was thus made fit to be a conqueror.*

—C.S. MAJOR GENERAL DANIEL H. HILL,
*Century Magazine,* FEBRUARY 1894

*To move swiftly, strike vigorously, and secure all the fruits*
*of victory, is the secret of successful war.*

—C.S. LIEUTENANT GENERAL THOMAS J. JACKSON, 1863,
G. F. R. HENDERSON, *Stonewall Jackson*
*and the American Civil War,* 1995

THE REBEL ARMY
is the legitimate property of the Army of the Potomac. They may as well pack up their haversacks
and make for Richmond.

—U.S. MAJOR GENERAL JOSEPH HOOKER,
*comment to reporter, April 30, 1863*

AT 6 P.M. THE ADVANCE WAS ORDERED. The enemy were taken by surprise, and fled after a brief resistance. General Rodes' men pushed forward with great vigor and enthusiasm, followed closely by the second and third lines. Position after position was carried, the guns captured, and every effort of the enemy to rally defeated by the impetuous rush of our troops.

—C.S. GENERAL ROBERT E. LEE,
*Official Report on the Battle of Chancellorsville, May 1863*

*Give General Jackson* my affectionate regards, and say to him—he has lost his left arm but I my right.

—C.S. GENERAL ROBERT E. LEE,
*message to Lt. General Thomas Jackson,*
*Chancellorsville, Virginia, May 2, 1863*

THE CHANCELLORSVILLE HOUSE AND THE woods surrounding it were wrapped in flames. In the midst of this awful scene, Gen. Lee . . . rode to the front of his advancing battalions. His presence was the signal for one of those uncontrollable outbursts of enthusiasm which none can appreciate who have not witnessed them. The fierce soldiers, with their faces blackened with the smoke of battle; the wounded, crawling with feeble limbs from the fury of the devouring flames, all seem possessed with a common impulse. One long, unbroken cheer, in which the feeble cry of those who lay helpless on the earth blended with the strong voices of those who still fought, rose high above the roar of battle . . . I thought it must have been from some such a scene that men in ancient days ascended to the dignity of the gods.

—A CONFEDERATE SOLDIER'S ACCOUNT OF LEE'S TRIUMPH AT CHANCELLORSVILLE, MAY 4, 1863, *Voices of the Civil War,* Time Life Books, 1996

*I see from the number of physicians* that you think my condition dangerous, but I thank God, if it is His will, that I am ready to go.

—C.S. LIEUTENANT GENERAL THOMAS J. JACKSON
ON HIS DEATHBED AT GUINEA STATION

*Let us pass over the river and rest under the shade of the trees.*

—C.S. LIEUTENANT GENERAL THOMAS J. JACKSON,
*last words, Guinea Station, Virginia, Sunday, May 10, 1863*

ANY VICTORY would be dear at such a price.

—C.S. GENERAL ROBERT E. LEE
ON THE DEATH OF STONEWALL JACKSON

THE CONFEDERATE ARMY could better have lost a corps of thirty thousand men, than Stonewall Jackson.

—U.S. MAJOR GENERAL
WINFIELD SCOTT HANCOCK,
*Johnny Reb and Billy Yank,* 1905

*My country is bleeding, my people are perishing around me. But I feel as a South Carolinian, I am bound to tell the North, go on! go on! Never falter, never abandon the principles which you have adopted!*

— ANGELINA GRIMKÉ,
abolitionist speech, May 14, 1863,
*The Grimké Sisters from South Carolina,* Gerda Lerner, 1967

*To tell the truth, I just lost confidence in Joe Hooker.*

—U.S. Major General Joseph E. Hooker,
comment after his defeat at Chancellorsville

*A deserted homestead is always a sad sight,* but here in the South we must look a little deeper than the surface, and then we see that every such overgrown plantation, and empty house, is a harbinger of freedom to the slaves, and every lover of his country, even if he have no feeling for the slaves themselves, should rejoice.

—U.S. Colonel Robert Gould Shaw,
*St. Simons Island, Georgia, June 9, 1863, Russell Duncan,*
Blue-Eyed Child of Fortune: The Civil War Letters
of Colonel Robert Gould Shaw, *1992*

# THE OLD FLAG
never touched the ground!

—SERGEANT WILLIAM H. CARNEY,
*54th Massachusetts Regiment, after the assault on
Fort Wagner, South Carolina, July 18, 1863,
Medal of Honor awarded, 1900*

*. . . a damned old goggled-eyed snapping turtle.*

—A SUBORDINATE'S DESCRIPTION OF
U.S. GENERAL GEORGE MEADE

*For a mile up and down the open fields* before us the splendid lines of the veterans of the Army of Northern Virginia swept down upon us. Their bearing was magnificent. They came forward with a rush, and how our men did yell, "Come on, Johnny, come on!"

—U.S. LIEUTENANT COLONEL RUFUS R. DAWES,
*6th Wisconsin, The Iron Brigade,*
*Gettysburg, Pennsylvania, July 1, 1863*

*The enemy is advancing in strong force, I will fight him inch by inch, and if driven into the town I will barricade the streets and hold him back as long as possible.*

—U.S. MAJOR GENERAL JOHN F. REYNOLDS,
*battlefield report, Gettysburg, July 1, 1863*

I THINK THIS IS the strongest position by nature on which to fight a battle that I ever saw.

—U.S. MAJOR GENERAL WINFIELD S. HANCOCK, *comment surveying the battlefield from Cemetery Ridge, Gettysburg, July 1, 1863*

*There are those damned black-hatted fellows again!*

—A CONFEDERATE SOLDIER ON SEEING THE ARRIVAL OF THE UNION "IRON BRIGADE" AT SEMINARY RIDE, GETTYSBURG, JULY 1, 1863

The Southern troops when charging, or to express their delight, always yell in a manner peculiar to themselves. The Yankee cheer is much more like ours; but the Confederate officers declare that the rebel yell has a peculiar merit, and always produces a salutary and useful effect upon their adversaries. A corps is sometimes spoken of as a "good yelling regiment."

—British Lieutenant Colonel
Arthur James Lyon Freemantle,
diary entry, July 2, 1863, Gettysburg,
*Three Months in the Southern States,* 1863

*Do you see those colors?* Take them!

—U.S. General Winfield S. Hancock,
*order to the 1st Minnesota regiment, Gettysburg, July 2, 1863*

*Hold that ground at all hazards.*

—U.S. COLONEL STRONG VINCENT,
ORDERS TO COLONEL JOSHUA LAWRENCE CHAMBERLAIN
AT LITTLE ROUND TOP, GETTYSBURG,
JULY 2, 1863

*The edge of the conflict swayed to and fro, with wild whirlpools and eddies. At times I saw around me more of the enemy than of my own men; gaps opening, swallowing, closing again with sharp convulsive energy. All around, a strange, mingled roar.*

—U.S. COLONEL JOSHUA LAWRENCE CHAMBERLAIN,
*20th Maine, at Little Round Top, Gettysburg,*
*July 2, 1863*

MY DEAD AND WOUNDED were nearly as great in number as those still on duty. They literally covered the ground. The blood stood in puddles in some places on the rocks; the ground was soaked with the blood of as brave men as ever fell on the red field of battle.

—C.S. COLONEL WILLIAM C. OATES, *15th Alabama, at Little Round Top, Gettysburg, July 2, 1863*

*The enemy is here,* and if we do not whip him, he will whip us.

—C.S. GENERAL ROBERT E. LEE, *comment to C.S. Lieutenant General James Longstreet at Gettysburg, Pennsylvania, July 2, 1863, quoted by Douglas Southall Freeman in* R. E. Lee: A Biography, *vol. 3, 1934*

THE HOARSE AND INDISTINGUISHABLE orders of commanding officers, the screaming and bursting of shells, canister and shrapnel as they tore through the struggling masses of humanity, the death screams of wounded animals, the groans of their human companions, wounded and dying and trampled underfoot by hurrying batteries, riderless horses and the moving lines of battle- a perfect Hell on earth, never, perhaps to be equaled, certainly not to be surpassed, nor ever to be forgotten in a man's lifetime. It has never been effaced from my memory, day or night, for fifty years.

—U.S. PRIVATE WILLIAM ARCHIBALD WAUGH,
*on the battle at Gettysburg, July 2, 1863*

GENERAL, I HAVE BEEN a soldier all my life. I have been with soldiers engaged in fights by couples, squads, companies, regiments, divisions and armies, and should know as well as anyone what soldiers can do. It is my opinion that no 15,000 men ever arrayed for battle can take that position.

— C.S. LIEUTENANT GENERAL JAMES LONGSTREET, *statement to General Lee before Pickett's Charge, July 3, 1863*

*A deathlike stillness then reigned over the field, and each army remained in breathless expectation of something yet to come still more dreadful.*

—C.S. BRIGADIER GENERAL A. L. LONG, describing midday at Gettysburg before Pickett's charge on July 3, 1863, *Memoirs of Robert E. Lee, His Military and Personal History*, 1886

*Longstreet rode slowly and alone* immediately in front of our entire line. He sat his large charger with a magnificent grace and composure I never before beheld. His bearing was to me the grandest moral spectacle of the war. I expected to see him fall every instant. Still he moved on, slowly and majestically, with a confidence, composure, self-possession and repressed power in every movement and look, *that fascinated me.*

—C.S. BRIGADIER GENERAL JAMES L. KEMPER, quoted by Larry Tag in *The Generals of Gettysburg: The Leaders of America's Greatest Battle,* 1998

*Up men, and to your posts! Don't forget today that you are from old Virginia!*

—C.S. MAJOR GENERAL E. GEORGE PICKETT, *rallying his division before the charge, Gettysburg, July 3, 1863*

It was the most beautiful thing I EVER SAW.

—A Union officer remembering Pickett's Charge

—

## Over on Cemetery Ridge, the Federals beheld a scene never before witnessed on this continent, —

*a scene which has never previously been enacted and can never take place again—an army forming in line of battle in full view, under their very eyes—charging across a space nearly a mile in length over fields of waving grain and anon of stubble and then a smooth expanse—moving with the steadiness of a dress parade, the pride and glory soon to be crushed by an overwhelming heartbreak.*

—C.S. Major General George E. Pickett, letter to his future wife Sallie, July 4, 1863

*There are times when a corps commander's life does not count.*

—U.S. Major General Winfield S. Hancock,
*Cemetery Ridge, Gettysburg, July 3, 1863*

___

# Tell General Hancock

for me that I have done him and done you all an injury which I shall regret the longest day I live.

—C.S. Lieutenant General Lewis A. Armistead,
*having fallen mortally wounded leading Pickett's Charge,
to U.S. Captain Henry H. Bingham who came to his aid,
Gettysburg, July 3, 1863*

*General Pickett, finding the battle broken* while the enemy was still reinforcing, called the troops off. There was no indication of panic. The broken files marched back in steady step. The effort was nobly made and failed from the blows that could not be fended.

—C.S. Lieutenant General James Longstreet, describing the end of Pickett's charge at Gettysburg, July 3, 1863, *Manassas to Appomattox: Memoirs of the Civil War in America,* 1896

*All this has been my fault.*

—C.S. General Robert E. Lee, upon riding to meet the survivors of Pickett's Charge, Gettysburg, July 3, 1863

WELL, IT IS ALL OVER NOW. THE BATTLE is lost, and many of us are prisoners, many are dead, many wounded, bleeding and dying. Your Soldier lives and mourns and but for you, my darling, he would rather, a million times rather, be back there with his dead, to sleep for all time in an unknown grave.

—C.S. MAJOR GENERAL GEORGE PICKETT, *letter to his fiancée, July 4, 1863*

I NEVER SAW TROOPS behave more magnificently than Pickett's division of Virginians did today in that grand charge upon the enemy. And if they had been supported as they were to have been—but, for some reason not yet explained to me, were not—we would have held the position and the day would have been ours.

—C.S. GENERAL ROBERT E. LEE,
*comment to C.S. brigadier general John D. Imboden, Gettysburg, July 3, 1863, quoted by Imboden in his memoirs,* Battles and Leaders of the Civil War, *vol. 3, 1888*

The battle is over, and although we did not succeed in pushing the enemy out of their strong position, I am sure they have not any thing to boast about. They have lost at least as many in killed and wounded as we have. We have taken more prisoners from them than they have from us. If that is not the case, why did they lay still all to-day and see our army going to the rear? An army that has gained a great victory follows it up while the enemy is badly crippled; but Meade, their commander, knows he has had as much as he gave, at least, if not more.

—C.S. Private Louis Leon,
*Diary of a Tar Heel Confederate Soldier,* 1913

*Great God! We had them in our grasp. We had only to stretch forth our hands and they were ours. Our army held the war in the hollow of their hand and would not close it.*

—PRESIDENT ABRAHAM LINCOLN,
ON LEARNING THE ARMY OF NORTHERN VIRGINIA
HAD ESCAPED ACROSS THE POTOMAC, JULY 14, 1863

*July 5th 1863—Glorious news!* We have won the victory, thank God, and the Rebel Army is fleeing to Virginia. We have news that Vicksburg has fallen. We have thousands of prisoners, and they seem stupefied with the news.

—U.S. FIRST LIEUTENANT ELISHA HUNT RHODES,
*diary entry, July 5, 1863,* All for the Union, *1985,*
*Robert Hunt Rhodes, editor*

# EVENTS HAVE SUCCEEDED ONE ANOTHER WITH DISASTROUS RAPIDITY.

*One brief month ago we were apparently at the point of success. Lee was in Pennsylvania threatening Harrisburg, and even Philadelphia. Vicksburg seemed to laugh all Grant's efforts to scorn. . . . All looked bright. Now the picture is just as somber as it was bright then. Lee failed at Gettysburg. . . . Vicksburg and Port Hudson capitulated. . . . It seems incredible that human power could effect such a change in so brief a space. Yesterday we rode on the pinnacle of success, today absolute ruin seems to be our portion.*

*The Confederacy totters to its destruction.*

—C.S. COLONEL JOSIAH GORGAS,
DIARY ENTRY, JULY 1863

*Gettysburg was the price the South paid for hav-ing Robert E. Lee as commander.*

—SHELBY FOOTE,
*quoted in* The Civil War, *Ken Burns, 1990*

*It is now conceded that all idea of British interven-tion is at an end. . . .* I want to hug the army of the Potomac. I want to get the whole army of Vicksburg drunk at my own expense. I want to fight some small man and lick him.

—HENRY BROOKS ADAMS,
*cheering the twin Union victories at
Gettysburg and Vicksburg in London*

## GETTYSBURG TODAY

is a place where gallant spirits still tell their story of high sacrifice and undying devotion. There is a cemetery, there are gentle ridges rolling unbroken toward the sunset, and here and there one can find spots where everything that is significant in the American dream speaks to today's world with an undying voice. Yet the battle was here and its presence is felt, and you cannot visit the place without feeling the echoes of what was once a proving ground for everything America believes in.

—BRUCE CATTON

War suits them. They are splendid riders, first rate shots and utterly reckless.

—U.S. BRIGADIER GENERAL WILLIAM T. SHERMAN, *comment on Southern cavalry, August 1863*

WHEN HOOD CAME WITH HIS SAD QUIXOTE face, the face of an old Crusader, who believed in his cause, his cross, and his crown, we were not prepared for such a man as a beau-ideal of the wild Texans. . . . The fierce light of Hood's eyes I can never forget.

—MARY CHESTNUT,
*diary entry on C.S. Lieutenant General John B. Hood,*
*August 1863*

*My son, remember that obedience is the soldier's first duty. If your commanding officer orders you to burn your neighbor's house down, and to sit on the ridge-pole till it falls in, do it.*

—JEFFERSON DAVIS,
*speech Missionary Ridge, Georgia, October 10, 1863*

*Better a generation should die on the battlefield, that their children may grow up in liberty and justice.*

—HARRIET BEECHER STOWE

With its cloud of skirmishers in advance,

With now the sound of a single shot snapping like a
   whip,

and now an irregular volley,

The swarming ranks press on and on, the dense brigades
   press on,

Gliterring dimly, toiling under the sun —
   the dust-cover'd men,

In columns rise and fall to the undulations of the ground,

With artillery interspers'd — the wheels rumble, the
   horses sweat,

As the army corps advances.

—WALT WHITMAN,
*General Burnside's Army Occupying Cumberland Gap,*
Harper's Weekly, *October 10, 1863*

*Four score and seven years ago* our fathers brought forth on this continent, a new nation, conceived in Liberty, and dedicated to the proposition that all men are created equal.

Now we are engaged in a great civil war, testing whether that nation, or any nation so conceived and so dedicated, can long endure. We are met on a great battle-field of that war. We have come to dedicate a portion of that field, as a final resting place for those who here gave their lives that that nation might live. It is altogether fitting and proper that we should do this.

But, in a larger sense, we can not dedicate — we can not consecrate — we can not hallow — this ground. The brave men, living and dead, who struggled here, have consecrated it, far above our poor power to add or detract. The world will little note, nor long remember what we say here, but it can never forget what they did here. It is for us the living, rather, to be dedicated here to the unfinished work which they who fought here have thus far so nobly advanced. It is rather for us to be here dedicated to the great task remaining before us — that from these honored dead we take increased devotion to that cause for which they gave the last full measure of devotion — that we here highly resolve that these dead shall not have died in vain — that this nation, under God, shall have a new birth of freedom — and that government of the people, by the people, for the people, shall not perish from the earth.

—ABRAHAM LINCOLN,
*Gettysburg Address, November 19, 1863*

# I FAILED, I FAILED,
and that is about all that can be said about it.

—ABRAHAM LINCOLN,
*comment after making his Gettysburg Address,*
*November 19, 1863*

WE PASS OVER THE SILLY REMARKS OF THE
President; for the credit of the Nation we are willing that
the veil of oblivion shall be dropped over them and that
they shall no more be repeated or thought of.

—*Harrisburg Patriot and Union*

*Could the most elaborate and splendid oration be more beautiful, more touching, more inspiring than those thrilling words of the President? They have in our humble judgment the charm and power of the very highest eloquence.*

*—Providence Journal*

*Not a sovereign in Europe,* however trained from the cradle for state pomps, and however prompted by statesmen and courtiers, could have uttered himself more regally than did Lincoln at Gettysburg.

—GOLDWIN SMITH

Indeed in this war more truly than in any other the spirit of lovely woman points the dart, hurls the javelin, ignites the mine, pulls the trigger, draws the lanyard and gives a fiercer truer temper to the blade in far more literal sense than the mere muscular aggressions of man.

—C.S. Major General J. E. B. Stuart,
*letter to his cousin Nannie, November 13, 1863*

SIX

# *The Road to*
# Appomattox:
# 1864–1865

# HITHERTO THE MARCH OF GRANT— THOUGH, IF IT BE ULTIMATELY SUCCESS- FUL, IT WILL BE CONSIDERED HEROIC— IS THE ADVANCE OF A PIECE OF MECHANISM.

*He sees no obstacles, and goes blindly and ruthlessly on. He trusts to nothing but superior numbers and hard fighting. The lives of his men are of no value. He throws them away by thousands, to gain half a mile of jungle. . . . At every step he fights at a disadvantage, on ground of the enemy's choosing.*

*But he fights on.*

—CHARLES MACKAY,
ARTICLE, *Times* (LONDON), FEBRUARY 28, 1864

I CAN ONLY SAY
that I am nothing but a poor sinner, trusting in
Christ alone for salvation.

—C.S. GENERAL ROBERT E. LEE,
*comment to army chaplains,*
*Orange, Virginia, February 1864*

*C.S.A. stands for corn, salt and apples,* the staple of
the Confederate soldier.

—CONFEDERATE PRIVATE,
*comment to a group of civilians*

*With this honor devolves upon you also a corresponding responsibility. As the country herein trusts you, so under God it will sustain you.*

—ABRAHAM LINCOLN,
*comment to Ulysses S. Grant at his promotion
to lieutenant general, March 12, 1864*

THAT MAN WILL FIGHT
us every day and every hour till the end of the war.

—C.S. LIEUTENANT GENERAL JAMES LONGSTREET,
*comment on U.S. Lieutenant General Ulysses S. Grant
taking command of all Union armies in March 1864,
quoted by Geoffrey C. Ward in* The Civil War:
An Illustrated History, *1990*

*General Grant* habitually wears an expression as if he had determined to drive his head through a brick wall and was about to do it.

—a Union private on Ulysses S. Grant

He had somehow, with all his modesty, the rare faculty of controlling his superiors as well as his subordinates. He outfaced Stanton, captivated the President, and even compelled acquiescence or silence from that dread source of paralyzing power, the Congressional Committee on the Conduct of the War.

—Joshua Lawrence Chamberlain, *speaking of General Grant*

*Lee's Army will be your objective point. Wherever Lee goes there you will go also.*

—U.S. LIEUTENANT GENERAL ULYSSES S. GRANT,
*orders to General George Meade, commander
of the Army of the Potomac, March 1864*

---

# THE ASSIGNMENT OF GENERAL GRANT TO THE COMMAND OF THE UNION ARMIES IN THE WINTER OF 1863-64

*gave presage of success from the start, for his eminent abilities
had already been proved, and besides, he was a tower of strength
to the government because he had the*

## confidence of the people.

—U.S. MAJOR GENERAL PHILIP H. SHERIDAN,
PERSONAL MEMOIRS OF P. H. SHERIDAN,
GENERAL UNITED STATES ARMY, VOL. 2, 1888

Grant had a gift given to few men; he could reach ordinary
people without condescending to them.

—WILLIAM S. MCFEELY, ON ULYSSES S. GRANT,
*quoted in* Grant: A Biography, 1981

He keeps his own counsel, padlocks his mouth, while his
countenance in battle or repose . . . indicates nothing—
*that is gives no expression of his feelings and no*
*evidence of his intentions.*

—CHARLES A. DANA,
*New York Tribune,* description of Ulysses S. Grant

*His imperturbability is amazing.*
*I am in doubt whether to call it*
**GREATNESS OR STUPIDITY.**

—James A. Garfield, on Ulysses S. Grant

*Quit thinking* about what Bobby Lee's gonna do to us
and start thinking about what we're going to do to him.

—U.S. Lieutenant General Ulysses S. Grant,
*orders to his generals after Lee's first attack*
*at Wilderness, May 1864*

I ALWAYS SHOOT AT PRIVATES. IT WAS THEY
who did the shooting and killing, and if I could kill or
wound a private, why, my chances were so much the better.
I always looked upon officers as harmless personages.

—C.S. PRIVATE SAM WATKINS

———

*That damned Yankee rifle that was loaded on
Sunday and fired all week!*

—A CONFEDERATE OFFICER,
AFTER AN ENCOUNTER WITH THE
7TH ILLINOIS VOLUNTEER INFANTRY
ARMED WITH HENRY RIFLES

In glades they meet skull after skull
Where pine cones lay - the rusted gun,
Green shoes full of bones, the mouldering coat
And cuddled up skeleton;
And scores of such. Some start as in dreams,
And comrades lost bemoan;
By the edge of those wilds Stonewall had charged-
But the year and the Man were gone.

—HERMAN MELVILLE,
"The Armies of the Wilderness,"
*Battle-Pieces and Aspects of the War,* 1866

*I'm ashamed of you, dodging that way!*
*They couldn't hit an elephant at this distance!*

—U.S. MAJOR GENERAL JOHN SEDGWICK,
WORDS TO HIS TROOPS MOMENTS BEFORE BEING SHOT DEAD
BY A CONFEDERATE SNIPER AT SPOTSYLVANIA COURTHOUSE,
MAY 9, 1964

NOW IT SEEMS STRANGE TO ME THAT WE do not receive the same pay and rations as the white soldiers. Do we not fill the same ranks? Do we not cover the same space of ground? Do we not take up the same length of ground in a graveyard that others do? The ball does not miss the black man and strike the white, nor the white and strike the black.

—U.S. PRIVATE EDWARD L. WASHINGTON,
*54th Massachusetts Regiment, letter, March 13, 1864*

One of the most effective ways of impeding the march of an army is *by cutting off its supplies;* and this is just as legitimate as to attack in the line of battle.

—C.S. COLONEL JOHN S. MOSBY,
*Mosby's War Reminiscences, 1887*

I AM NATURALLY ANTI-SLAVERY. IF SLAVERY is not wrong, nothing is wrong. I can not remember when I did not so think, and feel. And yet I have never understood that the Presidency conferred upon me an unrestricted right to act officially upon this judgment and feeling.

—ABRAHAM LINCOLN,
*letter to Albert Hodges, April 4, 1864,*
The Collected Works of Abraham Lincoln, *Roy P. Basler, 1953*

—

*There were probably but few men in the South who could have commanded successfully a separate detachment, in the rear of an opposing army and so near the border of hostilities, as long as he did without losing his entire command.*

—ULYSSES S. GRANT,
*on C.S. Colonel John S. Mosby*

*Go back! Go back!* Do your duty as I've done mine. I'd rather die than be whipped!

—C.S. Major General "Jeb" Stuart, orders to Confederate stragglers as he was being carried mortally wounded from the Battle of Yellow Tavern, May 11, 1864

I could have gone in and burned and killed right and left, I could capture Richmond, if I wanted, but I can't hold it. It isn't worth the men it would cost.

—U.S. Major General Philip H. Sheridan, *comment to a subordinate officer after the Battle of Yellow Tavern, Virginia, May 11, 1864*

I hate newspapermen. They come into camp and pick up their camp rumors and print them as facts. I regard them as spies, which, in truth, they are. *If I killed them all there would be news from Hell before breakfast.*

—U.S. BRIGADIER GENERAL WILLIAM T. SHERMAN

*I am out of money, we are all out of money, but we don't need money down here- Don't need anything but Men, Muskets, Ammunition, Hard Tack, Bacon and Letters from home.*

—LIEUTENANT COLONEL JAMES AUSTIN CONNOLLY, JUNE 20, 1864

THE MEN BENT DOWN AS THEY PUSHED forward, as if trying, as they were, to breast a tempest, and the files of men went down like rows of blocks or bricks pushed over by striking against one another.

—A UNION OFFICER'S DESCRIPTION OF THE ADVANCE AT COLD HARBOR, VIRGINIA, ON JUNE 3, 1864, *The Battle of Cold Harbor,* Gordon Rhea, 2001

*The dead covered more than five acres of ground about as thickly as they could be laid.*

—A CONFEDERATE DESCRIPTION OF THE UNION DEAD AT THE BATTLE OF COLD HARBOR, VIRGINIA, *June 1864*

I know that Mr. Davis thinks he can do a great many things other men would hesitate to attempt. For instance, he tried to do what God failed to do. He tried to make a soldier of Braxton Bragg, and you know the result. *It couldn't be done.*

—C.S. MAJOR GENERAL JOSEPH E. JOHNSTON,
COMMANDER OF THE ARMY OF TENNESSEE,
*just a few days before he was replaced by John Bell Hood by
Jefferson Davis, mid July 1864*

DAMN THE TORPEDOES.
FULL SPEED AHEAD!

—REAR ADMIRAL DAVID G. FARRAGUT,
ORDERS TO CAPTAIN OF THE U.S.S. *Hartford* DURING THE
BATTLE OF MOBILE BAY, AUGUST 5, 1864

# STAND FAST, MEN! STAND FAST!

—CORPORAL MILES OVIATT, U.S.M.C.,
*orders to his gun crew aboard the U.S.S.* Brooklyn, *under
fire from the Confederate ironclad* Tennessee *at Mobile Bay,
August 5, 1864*

*I*f *you don't have my army supplied, and keep it
supplied, we'll eat your mules up, sir.*

—U.S. BRIGADIER GENERAL WILLIAM T. SHERMAN,
*warning to an army quartermaster prior to the departure of
Sherman's army from Chattanooga toward Atlanta*

**IT IS NOT MERELY FOR TO-DAY, BUT FOR ALL TIME TO COME THAT WE SHOULD PERPETUATE FOR OUR CHILDREN'S CHILDREN THIS GREAT AND FREE GOVERNMENT, WHICH WE HAVE ENJOYED ALL OUR LIVES . . .**

*It is in order that each one of you may have through this free government which we have enjoyed, an open field and a fair chance for your industry, enterprise and intelligence: that you may all have equal privileges in the race of life, with all its desirable human aspirations. It is for this the struggle should be maintained, that we may not lose our birthright—not only for one, but for two or three years. The nation is worth fighting for,*
*to secure such an inestimable jewel.*

—ABRAHAM LINCOLN,
Speech to the 164th Ohio Regiment, August 22, 1864, *The Collected Works of Abraham Lincoln*, Roy P. Basler, 1953

*I am going to be beaten,* and unless some great change takes place, badly beaten.

—ABRAHAM LINCOLN,
*comment on his chances of reelection, August 1864*

*Atlanta is ours and fairly won.*

—U.S. BRIGADIER GENERAL
WILLIAM TECUMSEH SHERMAN,
TELEGRAM TO LINCOLN, SEPTEMBER 1, 1864

*Sherman will never go to hell, he'll flank the devil.*

—CONFEDERATE SOLDIER

## DARKEST OF ALL

Decembers ever has my life known, sitting here by the embers, stunned, helpless, alone.

—MARY CHESTNUT,
*diary entry after the fall of Atlanta*

———

*Until we can repopulate Georgia,* it is useless for us to occupy it; but the utter destruction of its roads, houses and people will cripple their military resources. I can make this march, *and make Georgia howl.*

—U.S. MAJOR GENERAL WILLIAM T. SHERMAN,
*telegram sent to General Ulysses S. Grant at Atlanta, Georgia, September 9, 1864*

THE NAME OF THE CAPTOR OF ATLANTA,
if he fails now, will become the scoff of mankind and the
humiliation of the United States for all time. If he succeeds
it will be written on the tablet of fame.

—*London Herald*

—

War is cruelty, and you cannot refine it.

—U.S. MAJOR GENERAL WILLIAM T. SHERMAN,
LETTER, SEPTEMBER 12, 1864

—

*I know the hole he went in at, but I can't tell you
what hole he will come out of.*

—ABRAHAM LINCOLN,
*remark when asked the destination of
Sherman's March to the Sea*

*You say we insulted your flag.* The truth is we fired upon it, and those who fought under it, when you came to our doors upon the mission of subjugation.

—C.S. GENERAL JOHN B. HOOD,
*letter to U.S. Major General William T. Sherman,*
*September 12, 1864*

*You can not have free government without elections, and if the rebellion could force us to forgo, or postpone a national election, it might fairly claim to have already conquered and ruined us.*

—ABRAHAM LINCOLN,
*informal speech, November 10, 1864*

# SURRENDER MEANS THAT THE HISTORY OF THIS HEROIC STRUGGLE WILL BE WRITTEN BY THE ENEMY;

*that our youth will be trained by Northern school teachers; will learn from Northern school books their version of the War; will be impressed by all the influences of history and education to regard our gallant dead as traitors, and our maimed veterans as fit subjects for derision.*

—C.S. MAJOR GENERAL PAT CLEBURNE

If we are to die, let us die like men.

—C.S. MAJOR GENERAL PATRICK R. CLEBURNE, *reply to Brigadier Daniel C. Govan who opposed advancing against Union entrenchments at the Battle of Franklin, Tennessee, November 30, 1864*

IT WAS THE GRANDEST SIGHT I EVER SAW when our army marched over the hill and reached the open field base. Each division unfolded itself into a single line of battle with as much steadiness as if forming for dress parade . . . The men were tired, hungry, footsore, ragged, and many of them barefooted, but their spirit was admirable.

—C.S. JAMES D. PORTER,
*describing the moment before the attack at*
*Franklin, Tennessee, November 30, 1864*

*Every room was filled, every bed* had two poor, bleeding fellows, every spare space, niche, and corner under the stairs, in the hall, everywhere. And when the noble old house could hold no more, the yard was appropriated *until the wounded and dead filled that.*

—JOHN AND CARRIE MCGAVOCK
*describing their Carnton estate after the*
*Battle of Franklin, Tennessee, November 30, 1864*

FRANKLIN IS THE BLACKEST page in the history of the War of the Lost Cause. It was the bloodiest battle of modern times in any war. It was the finishing stroke to the Independence of the Southern Confederacy. I was there. I saw it.

—C.S. PRIVATE SAM WATKINS

*When we got within 800 yards. They opened terrific fire of shot, shell, grape and canister, and when the troops got to within 400 yards. The musketry united with the cannon and it appeared to come by the millions. I cannot see how any human being could live 2 moments in such a place.*

—C.S. 1ST LIEUTENANT WILLIAM HARVEY BERRYHILL, *letter to wife, December 1, 1864, Franklin, Tennessee,* The Gentle Rebel, *Mary Miles Jones and Leslie Jones Martin (ed.)*

*I beg to present you* as a Christmas gift the city of Savannah, with one hundred and fifty heavy guns and plenty of ammunition; also about twenty-five thousand bales of cotton.

—U.S. BRIGADIER GENERAL
WILLIAM TECUMSEH SHERMAN,
*telegram to Abraham Lincoln, December 22, 1864*

*Let us say to every Negro who wishes to go into the ranks,
"Go and fight—you are free."*

— JUDAH P. BENJAMIN,
CONFEDERATE STATES SECRETARY OF STATE, ON BLACKS
VOLUNTEERING TO FIGHT FOR THE CONFEDERACY, 1864

YOU CANNOT MAKE SOLDIERS OF SLAVES,
or slaves of soldiers. The day you make a soldier of them is the
beginning of the end of the Revolution. And if slaves seem
good soldiers, then our whole theory of slavery is wrong.

—C.S. MAJOR GENERAL HOWELL COBB,
*quoted from* Battle Cry of Freedom,
*James M. McPherson, 1988*

*Peace on Earth, Good will to men* should prevail. We certainly would preserve the peace if they would go home and let us alone ...

—C.S. PRIVATE JOHNNY GREEN,
*letter home, December 25, 1864*

THE TRUTH IS, the whole army is burning with an insatiable desire to wreak vengeance upon South Carolina. I almost tremble at her fate, but feel she deserves all that seems in store for her.

—U.S. MAJOR GENERAL WILLIAM T. SHERMAN,
*February 1865*

*With malice toward none; with charity for all; with firmness in the right, as God gives us to see the right, let us strive on to finish the work we are in; to bind up the nation's wounds; to care for him who shall have borne the battle, and for his widow, and his orphan—to do all which may achieve and cherish a just and lasting peace, among ourselves, and with all nations.*

—ABRAHAM LINCOLN,
*Second Inaugural Address, Washington, D.C., March 4, 1865*

RICHMOND HAS FALLEN — AND I HAVE no heart to write about it . . . They are too many for us. Everything lost in Richmond, even our archives. Blue-black is our horizon.

—MARY CHESTNUT, DIARY ENTRY, APRIL 1865

**Fondly do we hope—fervently do we pray—that this mighty scourge of war may speedily pass away.**

*Yet, if God wills that it continue until all the wealth piled by the bondsman's two hundred and fifty years of unrequited toil shall be sunk, and until every drop of blood drawn with the lash shall be paid by another drawn with the sword, as was said three thousand years ago, so still it must be said:*

*"The judgments of the Lord are true, and righteous altogether."*

—Abraham Lincoln,
letter to Amanda Hall, March 20, 1865

*If the Confederacy falls, there should be written on its tombstone: Died of a Theory.*

—JEFFERSON DAVIS

THE ART OF WAR IS SIMPLE enough. Find out where your enemy is. Get at him as soon as you can. Strike at him as hard as you can and as often as you can, and keep moving on.

—U.S. MAJOR GENERAL ULYSSES S. GRANT,
*attributed*

IF CENTRALISM IS ULTIMATELY TO PREVAIL; if our entire system of free Institutions as established by our common ancestors is to be subverted, and an Empire is to be established in their stead; if that is to be the last scene of the great tragic drama now being enacted: then, be assured, that we of the South will be acquitted, not only in our own consciences, but in the judgment of mankind, of all responsibility for so terrible a catastrophe, and from all guilt of so great a crime against humanity.

—ALEXANDER STEPHENS

*Men, the salvation of the army is in your keep. Don't surrender this fort!*

—C.S. BRIGADIER NATHANIEL H. HARRIS, *Battle of Fort Gregg, Petersburg, Virginia, April 2, 1865*

I WANT NO ONE
punished. Treat them liberally all around. We want
those people to return to their allegiance to the
Union and submit to the laws.

—ABRAHAM LINCOLN,
*message to General Ulysses S. Grant, General William T.*
*Sherman, and Admiral David D. Porter, March 28, 1865*

General: I have received your note of this date. Though
not entertaining the opinion you express of the hope-
lessness of further resistance on the part of the Army
of Northern Virginia, I reciprocate your desire to avoid
useless effusion of blood, and therefore, *before consider-*
*ing your proposition, ask the terms you will offer on*
*condition of its surrender.*

—C.S. GENERAL ROBERT E. LEE,
*letter to U.S. General Ulysses S. Grant,*
*Appomattox, Virginia, April 7, 1865*

*There is nothing left but to go to General Grant;*
*and I would rather die a thousand deaths.*

—C.S. General Robert E. Lee,
April 8, 1865, quoted by Edward Lee Childe
in *Life and Campaigns of General Lee,* 1975

## Country be damned.

There is no country. There has been no country, General, for a year or more. You are the country to these men. They have fought for you . . . there are thousands left who will die for you.

—C.S. General Henry A. Wise Jr.,
*said to General Robert E. Lee before his surrender at*
*Appomattox, Virginia, April 9, 1865*

*How easily I could be rid of this, and be at rest! I have only to ride along the line and all will be over! . . . But it is our duty to live. What will become of the women and children of the South if we are not here to protect them?*

—GENERAL ROBERT E. LEE,
*Appomattox, Virginia, April 9, 1865*

*Deep sadness,* overmastered by deeper strength.

—A UNION SOLDER DESCRIBING LEE AT
APPOMATTOX COURT HOUSE, VIRGINIA, MAY 9, 1865

# The meeting of Lee and Grant at Appomattox was the momentous epoch of the century.

*It marked greater changes, uprooted a grander and nobler civilization, and, in the emancipation of one race and the impoverishment of another, it involved vaster consequences than had ever followed*

## *the fall of a dynasty or the wreck of an empire.*

—C.S. Major General John B. Gordon,
*Reminiscences of the Civil War*, 1904

IF ONE ARMY DRANK THE JOY OF VICTORY, and the other the bitter draught of defeat, it was a joy moderated by the recollection of the cost at which it had been purchased, and a defeat mollified by the consciousness of many triumphs. If the victors could recall a Malvern Hill, an Antietam, a Gettysburg, a Five Forks, the vanquished could recall a Manassas, a Fredericksburg, a Chancellorsville, a Cold Harbor.

—WILLIAM SWINTON,
*New York Times*

*We have fought this fight* as long as, and as well as, we know how. We have been defeated. For us, as a Christian people, there is now but one course to pursue. We must accept the situation. These men must go home and plant a crop, and *we must proceed to build up our country on a new basis.*

—C.S. General Robert E. Lee,
*comment to C.S. Brigadier General Edward P. Alexander,*
*April 9, 1965, quoted by Charles Francis Adams in* Lee at
Appomattox, *1902*

# . . . On they come, with the old swinging route step and swaying battle flags. In the van, the proud Confederate ensign.

*Before us in proud humiliation stood the embodiment of manhood; men whom neither toils and sufferings, nor the fact of death could bend from their resolve; standing before us now, thin, worn, and famished, but erect, and with eyes looking level into ours, waking memories that bound us together as no other bond; was not such manhood to be welcomed back into a Union so tested and assured? On our part not a sound of trumpet more, nor roll of drum; not a cheer, nor word, nor whisper or vain-glorying, nor motion of man, but an awed stillness rather, and breath-holding,*

*as if it were the passing of the dead!*

—U.S. MAJOR GENERAL
JOSHUA LAWRENCE CHAMBERLAIN,
ON THE SURRENDER OF THE ARMY OF
NORTHERN VIRGINIA, APPOMATTOX, APRIL 12, 1865

ONE OF THE KNIGHTLIEST
soldiers of the Federal army, General Joshua L.
Chamberlain of Maine, who afterward served
with distinction as governor of his State, called his
troops into line, and as my men marched in front of
them, the veterans in blue gave a soldierly salute to
those vanquished heroes—a token of respect from
Americans to Americans, a final and fitting tribute
from Northern to Southern chivalry.

—C.S. Major General John B. Gordon,
writing on the surrender of the Army of
Northern Virginia at Appomattox, 1865,
*Reminiscences of the Civil War*, 1904

*I felt like anything rather than rejoicing* at the down-fall of a foe who had fought so long and valiantly, and who had suffered so much for a cause, though that cause was, I believe, one of the worst for which a people ever fought, and one for which there was the least excuse.

—U.S. LIEUTENANT GENERAL ULYSSES S. GRANT,
*recalling the surrender at Appomattox Court House*

*America has no north, no south, no east, no west. The sun rises over the hills and sets over the mountains, the compass just points up and down, and we can laugh now at the absurd notion of there being a north and a south. We are one and undivided.*

—C.S. PRIVATE SAM WATKINS

THEY HAVE ACHIEVED BY STARVATION what they could never win by their valor, and nor have they taken a single town in the South except Vicksburg that we have not evacuated.

—MARY CUSTIS LEE,
*letter to cousin after the surrender at Appomattox*

We are scattered, stunned; the remnant of heart left alive is filled with brotherly hate . . . Whose fault? Everybody blamed somebody else. Only the dead heroes left stiff and stark on the battle-field escape.

—MARY CHESTNUT

I HAVE NEVER on the field of battle sent you where I was unwilling to go myself, nor would I now advise you to a course which I felt myself unwilling to pursue. You have been good soldiers. You can be good citizens. Obey the laws, preserve your honor, and the government to which you have surrendered can afford to be and will be magnanimous.

—C.S. LIEUTENANT NATHAN BEDFORD FORREST,
*orders to his men upon hearing the war had ended*

*In the good providence of God apparent failure often proves a blessing. . . . My trust is in the mercy and wisdom of a kind Providence, who ordereth all things for our good.*

—C.S. GENERAL ROBERT E. LEE

*Sometimes I examine myself thoroughly* and I will always come to the conclusion that I am not such a bad man at last as I am looked upon. God will give me justice if I am to be punished for the opinions of other people, who do not know my heart I cant help it.

—Stand Watie, First Cherokee Mounted Rifles, *comment to his wife, April 24, 1864*

*"Who is dead in the White House?"'*
*demanded of one of the soldiers, "The President,"*
*was his answer; "he was killed by an assassin."*

—Abraham Lincoln,
recounting his dream on the night of April 11, 1865,
*Recollections of Abraham Lincoln 1847–1865,*
Ward Hill Lamon, 1994

*C*rook, do you know I believe there are men who want to take my life? And I have no doubt they will do it. . . . I know no one could do it and escape alive. But if it is to be done, it is impossible to prevent it.

—Abraham Lincoln,
*comment to bodyguard, William H. Crook,*
*April 14, 1865*

*Sic semper tyrannis!* The South is avenged!

—JOHN WILKES BOOTH,
AFTER SHOOTING ABRAHAM LINCOLN AND LEAPING TO THE
STAGE AT FORD'S THEATRE, WASHINGTON, D.C., FRIDAY
APRIL 14, 1865 (THUS ALWAYS TO TYRANTS!)

# UNTIL TODAY NOTHING WAS EVER THOUGHT OF SACRIFICING TO OUR COUNTRY'S WRONGS....

*I can never repent it, though we hated to kill. Our country owed all her troubles to him, and God simply made me the instrument of his punishment. The country is not what it was. This forced Union is not what I have loved. I care not what becomes of me.*

*I have no desire to outlive my country.*

—JOHN WILKES BOOTH,
DIARY ENTRY, APRIL 1865

# USELESS, USELESS!

—JOHN WILKES BOOTH,
*dying words gazing at his own hands, April 16, 1865*

NOW HE BELONGS TO THE AGES.

—SECRETARY OF WAR EDWIN STANTON,
*at the moment of the President's death,*
*Saturday, April 15, 1865*

*The last day he lived was the happiest of his life.*

—MARY TODD LINCOLN,
*comment to Reverend Noyes W. Miner, "The Later Life and*
*Religious Sentiments of Abraham Lincoln," a lecture by*
*Rev. J. A. Reed,* Scribner's Monthly, *July 1873*

O Captain! my Captain, our fearful trip is done,
The ship has weather'd every rack,
the prize we sought is won,
The port is near, the bells I hear,
the people all exulting,
While follow eyes the steady keel,
the vessel grim and daring;
      But O heart! heart! heart!
       O the bleeding drops of red,
        Where on the deck my Captain lies,
         Fallen cold and dead.

—Walt Whitman, *Leaves of Grass*, 1881

A RETURN TO THE UNION WILL BRINGS ALL the horrors of war, coupled with all the degradation that can be inflicted on a conquered people. . . . If I can serve you or my country by any further fighting you have only to tell me so.

—C.S. LIEUTENANT GENERAL WADE HAMPTON,
*message to Confederate president Jefferson Davis,
April 22, 1865*

———

*Abandon your animosities
and make your sons Americans.*

—C.S. GENERAL ROBERT E. LEE, 1865,
"HE LOST A WAR AND WON IMMORTALITY,"
LOUIS REDMOND

NEITHER SLAVERY nor involuntary servitude, except as a punishment for crime whereof the party shall have been duly convicted, shall exist within the United States, or any place subject to their jurisdiction.

—AMENDMENT XIII OF THE UNITED STATES CONSTITUTION, *ratified 1865*

*The gentleman does not needlessly and unnecessarily remind an offender of a wrong he may have committed against him. He cannot only forgive, he can forget; and he strives for that nobleness of self and mildness of character which impart sufficient strength to let the past be but the past. A true man of honor feels humbled himself when he cannot help humbling others.*

—ROBERT E. LEE

*Thus ended the great American Civil War,* which upon the whole must be considered the noblest and least avoidable of all the great mass conflicts of which till then there was record.

— SIR WINSTON CHURCHILL,
*A History of the English-Speaking Peoples*

# SEVEN

# On Lincoln

If any personal description of me is thought desirable, it may be said I am, in height, six feet, four inches, nearly; lean in flesh, weighing, on average, one hundred and eighty pounds; dark complexion, with course black hair, and gray eyes—no other marks or brands recollected.

—Abraham Lincoln,
*Autobiographical Statement for* Chester County Times,
*December 1859*

⸺

*Without a doubt the greatest man of the rebellion times, the one matchless among forty millions for the peculiar difficulties of the period, was Abraham Lincoln.*

—C.S. Lieutenant General James Longstreet,
*Battles and Leaders of the Civil War,* vol. 2, 1888

## Public sentiment

is everything. With public sentiment, nothing can
fail; without it nothing can succeed.

—Abraham Lincoln,
Lincoln-Douglas Debate at Ottawa, Illinois,
August 21, 1858, *The Collected Works of Abraham
Lincoln*, edited by Roy P. Basler, volume III, 1953

*What is conservatism?* Is it not adherence to the old and
tried, against the new and untried?

—Abraham Lincoln,
*Cooper Institute Address, New York City,
February 27, 1860*

# To this place, and the kindness of these people, I owe everything.

*Here I have lived a quarter of a century, and have passed from a young to an old man. Here my children have been born, and one is buried. I now leave, not knowing when, or whether ever, I may return, with a task before me greater than that which rested upon Washington.*

*Without the assistance of the Divine Being who ever attended him, I cannot succeed. With that assistance I cannot fail.*

—Abraham Lincoln,
Farewell Address at the Great Western Depot
in Springfield, Illinois, February 11, 1861

*All honor to Jefferson—to the man who, in the concrete pressure of a struggle for national independence by a single people, had the coolness, forecast, and capacity to introduce into a merely revolutionary document, an abstract truth, applicable to all men and all times, and so embalm it there, that to-day, and in all coming days, it shall be a rebuke and a stumbling-block to the very harbingers of re-appearing tyranny and oppression.*

—ABRAHAM LINCOLN,
*letter to H. L. Pierce, April 6, 1859*

IF THE UNITED STATES be not a government proper, but an association of States in the nature of contract merely, can it, as a contract, be peaceably unmade by less than all the parties who made it? One party to a contract may violate it — break it, so to speak — but does it not require all to lawfully rescind it?

—U.S. PRESIDENT ABRAHAM LINCOLN,
*March 4, 1861,*
*First Inaugural Address*

IT IS TRUE THAT WHILE I HOLD MYSELF without mock modesty the humblest of all the individuals that have ever been elevated to the Presidency, I have a more difficult task to perform than any one of them.

—ABRAHAM LINCOLN,
*speech to the New York State Legislature,*
*Albany, New York, February 18, 1861*

*Unquestionably, Western man though he may be, and Kentuckian by birth, President Lincoln is the essential representative of all Yankees, and the veritable specimen, physically, of what the world seems determined to regard as our characteristic qualities.*

—NATHANIEL HAWTHORNE,
"Chiefly About War Matters" from *Atlantic Monthly,*
July 1862

I see the President almost every day. I see very plainly Abraham Lincoln's dark brown face with its deep-cut lines, the eyes always to me with a deep latent sadness in the expression. None of the artists or pictures has caught the deep, though subtle and indirect expression of this man's face. There is something else there. One of the great portrait painters of two or three centuries ago is needed.

—WALT WHITMAN

OUR POPULAR GOVERNMENT HAS OFTEN been called an experiment. Two points in it our people have already settled—the successful establishing and the successful administering of it. One still remains—its successful maintenance against a formidable internal attempt to overthrow it. It is now for them to demonstrate to the world that those who can fairly carry an election can also suppress a rebellion; that ballots are the rightful and peaceful successors of bullets; and that when ballots have fairly and constitutionally decided, there can be no successful appeal back to bullets; that there can no be no successful appeal except to ballots themselves, at succeeding elections. Such will be a great lesson of peace; teaching men that what they cannot take by an election neither can they take by a war; teaching all the folly of being the beginners of a war.

—ABRAHAM LINCOLN,
*address to Congress, July 4, 1861*

I don't like to hear cut-and-dried sermons. No—
*when I hear a man preach, I like to see him act as
if he were fighting bees.*

—Abraham Lincoln

If ever there was
a diamond in the rough, or a good fruit enclosed in
shabby husk, it was Abraham Lincoln.

—U.S. Brigadier General Erasmus D. Keyes,
*Fifty Years' Observation of Men and Events,
Civil and Military,* 1884

# LEAVE NOTHING FOR TOMORROW WHICH CAN BE DONE TODAY.

—ABRAHAM LINCOLN

*No other name* has such electric power on every true heart, from Maine to Mexico, as the name of Lincoln. If Washington is the most revered, Lincoln is the best loved man that ever trod this continent.

—REVEREND DR. THEODORE L. CUYLER

I DON'T S'POSE
anybody on earth likes gingerbread better'n I do—
and gets less'n I do.

—ABRAHAM LINCOLN,
quoted by Carl Sandburg
*Abraham Lincoln: The Prairie Years,* 2005

*Mr. Lincoln was a humorist so full of fun
that he could not keep it all in.*

—JAMES B. FRY,
FORMER ADJUTANT-GENERAL UNITED STATES ARMY

... *his laugh stood by itself.* The neigh of a wild horse on his native prairie is not more undisguised and hearty.

—Francis B. Carpenter,
*The Inner Life of Abraham Lincoln:*
*Six Months at the White House,* 1866

I was never more quickly or more completely put at ease in the presence of a great man, than in that of Abraham Lincoln ... I at once felt myself in the present of an honest man—one whom I could love, honor and trust without reserve or doubt.

—Frederick Douglass,
*on meeting Lincoln for the first time*

*The London Times is one of the greatest powers in the world—in fact, I don't know anything which has much more power,—except perhaps the Mississippi. I am glad to know you as its minister.*

—ABRAHAM LINCOLN,
*at meeting William Howard Russell*
*at the White House in 1861*

**THERE ARE NO ACCIDENTS
IN MY PHILOSOPHY.**
*Every effect must have its cause. The past is the cause of the present, and the present will be the cause of the future. All these are links in the endless chain*

## stretching from the finite to the infinite.

—*Abraham Lincoln,*
quoted in *Herndon's Life of Lincoln*
by William H. Herndon and Jesse W. Weik, 1983

THE DOGMAS OF THE quiet past are inadequate to the stormy present. As our case is new, so we must think anew, and act anew. We must disenthrall ourselves, and then we shall save our country.

—ABRAHAM LINCOLN,
*Annual Message to Congress, December 1, 1862*

THEY SAY I TELL A GREAT MANY STORIES; *I reckon I do, but I have found in the course of a long experience that common people, take them as they run, are more easily informed through the medium of a broad illustration than in any other way, and as to what the hypercritical few may think,* I don't care.

—ABRAHAM LINCOLN, AS QUOTED IN CONVERSATION TO CHAUNCEY M. DEPEW, NEW YORK SENATOR

*Mr. Lincoln's wit and mirth* will give him a passport to the thoughts and hearts of millions who would take no interest in the sterner and more practical parts of his character.

— George S. Boutwell,
*Secretary of the United States Treasury*

*Viewing the man from the genuine abolitionist ground, Mr. Lincoln seemed cold, tardy, weak and unequal to the task. But, viewing him from the sentiments of his people, which as a statesman he was bound to respect, then his actions were swift, bold, radical and decisive. Taking the man in the whole, balancing the tremendous magnitude of the situation, and the necessary means to ends, Infinite Wisdom has rarely sent a man into the world more perfectly suited to his mission than Abraham Lincoln.*

—Frederick Douglass

I BELIEVE IT IS AN ESTABLISHED MAXIM IN morals that he who makes an assertion without knowing whether it is true or false, is guilty of falsehood; and the accidental truth of the assertion, does not justify or excuse him.

—ABRAHAM LINCOLN,
*letter to Allen N. Ford, August 11, 1846*

*It is hard, hard, hard to have him die!*

—ABRAHAM LINCOLN,
ON THE DEATH OF HIS ELEVEN-YEAR-OLD SON
WILLIAM WALLACE LINCOLN, FEBRUARY 20, 1862

# My earlier views

of the unsoundness of the Christian scheme of salvation and the human origin of the scriptures have become clearer and stronger with advancing years, and I see no reason for thinking I shall ever change them.

—Abraham Lincoln,
*1862 letter to Judge J. S. Wakefield, after the death of Willie Lincoln, February 20, 1862*

*In the present civil war* it is quite possible that God's purpose is something different from the purpose of either party.

—Abraham Lincoln, September 2, 1862,
*Collected Works of Abraham Lincoln,* 1953

*If there be those who would not save the Union unless they could at the same time destroy slavery, I do not agree with them.*

## MY PARAMOUNT OBJECT IN THIS STRUGGLE IS TO SAVE THE UNION, AND IS NOT EITHER TO SAVE OR DESTROY SLAVERY.

*If I could save the Union without freeing any slave, I would do it; and if I could save it by freeing all the slaves, I would do it; and if I could save it by freeing some and leaving others alone, I would also do that. What I do about slavery and the colored race, I do because I believe it helps to save the Union; and what I forbear, I forbear because I do not believe it would help save the Union.*

—ABRAHAM LINCOLN
"EXECUTIVE MANSION" REPLY TO HORACE GREELEY'S
*New York Tribune* EDITORIAL "THE PRAYER OF TWENTY
MILLIONS," AUGUST 22, 1862

*I have not permitted myself,* gentlemen, to conclude that I am the best man in the country; but I am reminded in this connection of a story of an old Dutch farmer, who remarked to a companion once that it was not best to swap horses when crossing a stream.

—Abraham Lincoln,
*reply to National Union League, June 9, 1864*

*I* *have always thought "Dixie" one of the best tunes I ever heard.*

—Abraham Lincoln,
*April 10, 1865*

MY CONCERN IS NOT whether God is on our side. My greatest concern is to be on God's side, as God is always right.

—ABRAHAM LINCOLN

WE CANNOT BRING OURSELVES TO THINK

*that Mr. Lincoln has done anything that would furnish a precedent dangerous to our liberties, or in any way overstep the just limits of his constitutional discretion.*

*If his course has been unusual, it was because the danger was equally so.*

—RUSSELL JAMES LOWELL,
*North American Review,*
January 1864

*Gold is good in its place; but living, brave, patriotic men, are better than gold.*

—ABRAHAM LINCOLN

*Must I shoot a simple-minded soldier boy* who deserts, while I must not touch a hair of the wily agitator who induces him to desert? I think that in such a case to silence the agitator and save the boy is not only constitutional but withal a great mercy.

—ABRAHAM LINCOLN,
*defending his detention of antiwar politician*
*Clement Vallandigham*

*You say you will not fight to free negroes. Some of them seem willing to fight for you; but, no matter. Fight you, then exclusively to save the Union.*

—ABRAHAM LINCOLN,
letter to James Conkling, August 26, 1863,
*The Collected Works of Abraham Lincoln*, Roy P. Basler, 1953

I LONG AGO MADE UP MY MIND THAT IF anybody wants to kill me, he will do it. If I wore a shirt of mail and kept myself surrounded by a bodyguard, it would be all the same. There are a thousand ways of getting at a man if it is desirable that he should be killed. Besides, in this case, it seems to me, the man who would come after me would be just as objectionable to my enemies.

—ABRAHAM LINCOLN,
*remark to Noah Brooks, spring 1863*

*A* great man, tender of heart, strong of nerve, boundless patience and broadest sympathy, with no motive apart from his country.

—Frederick Douglass

My wife is as handsome as when she was a girl, and I a poor nobody then, fell in love with her, and what is more, I have never fallen out.

—Abraham Lincoln,
from *Abraham and Mary Lincoln: A House Divided*

SOME OF MY GENERALS COMPLAIN THAT I impair discipline and subordination in the army by my pardons and respites, but it makes me rested after a day's hard work if I can find some good excuse for saving a man's life, and I go to bed happy as I think how joyous the signing of my name will make him and his family and friends.

—ABRAHAM LINCOLN,
*remark to Schuyler Colfax, Speaker of the House of Representatives, 1864*

I claim not to have controlled events,
but confess plainly that events have controlled me.

—ABRAHAM LINCOLN,
LETTER TO ALBERT G. HODGES, APRIL 4, 1864,
*The Collected Works of Abraham Lincoln*
EDITED BY ROY P. BASLER, VOLUME VII, 1953

# I AM A TIRED MAN.
Sometimes I think I am the tiredest man on earth.

—ABRAHAM LINCOLN,
*comment after his second inaugural address,*
*March 4, 1865, quoted by Geoffrey C. Ward,*
The Civil War: An Illustrated History, *1990*

---

*Both parties deprecated war; but one of them would make war rather than let the nation survive; and the other would accept war rather than let it perish. And the war came.*

—ABRAHAM LINCOLN,
*Second Inaugural Address, March 4, 1865*

*Tell your father, the rascal,* that I forgive him for the sake of that kiss and those bright eyes.

—ABRAHAM LINCOLN,
*comment to the baby son of C.S. Major General George Pickett after stopping by his home in Richmond, April 1865, quoted by Sallie Corbell Pickett*

PROBABLY NO RULER EVER MADE A MORE profoundly and peculiarly Christian impression on the mind of the world than Lincoln. In his religious faith two leading ideas were prominent from first to last— man's helplessness, both as to strength and wisdom, and God's helpfulness in both.

—HARRIET BEECHER STOWE,
*Men of Our Times; or Leading Patriots of the Day,* 1868

*I would rather be assassinated than see
a single star removed from the American flag.*

—Abraham Lincoln

Mary, I consider this day, the war, has come to a close . . . we must both be more cheerful in the future — between the war and the loss of our darling Willie — we have both been very miserable.

—Abraham Lincoln,
comment to Mary Todd Lincoln, April 14, 1865,
*Team of Rivals: The Political Genius of Abraham
Lincoln*, Doris Kearns Goodwin, 2005

*W*hat does anyone want to assassinate me for? If any one wants to do so, he can do it day or night if he is ready to give his life for mine. It is nonsense.

—Abraham Lincoln,
*comment to his bodyguard Marshal Ward Hill Lamon,*
*April 14, 1865, quoted by Colonel Alexander K. McClure,*
Lincoln's Yarns and Stories, *1904*

It was no accident that planted Lincoln on a Kentucky farm, half way between the lakes and the Gulf. The association there had substance in it. Lincoln belonged just where he was put. *If the Union was to be saved, it had to be a man of such an origin that should save it.*

—Mark Twain,
*quoted in* New York Times, *January 13, 1907*

# That speech, uttered at the field of Gettysburg . . .

*and now sanctified by the martyrdom of its author, is a monumental act. In the modesty of his nature he said "the world will little note, nor long remember what we say here; but it can never forget what they did here." He was mistaken. The world at once noted what he said, and will never cease to remember it. The battle itself was less important than the speech.*

## *Ideas are always more than battles.*

—Charles Sumner

No one will ever know what Abraham Lincoln would have done . . . Thinking to destroy a tyrant, Booth managed to destroy a man who was trying to create a broader freedom for all men; with him, he destroyed also the chance for a transcendent peace without malice and with charity for all. Over the years, many people paid a high price for this moment of violence.

—Bruce Catton,
*"Never Call Retreat"*

EIGHT

# Remembrance

# THE GLORY OF THIS LAND HAS BEEN ITS CAPACITY FOR TRANSCENDING THE MORAL EVILS OF OUR PAST.

*For example, the long struggle of minority citizens for equal rights, once a source of disunity and civil war, is now a point of pride for all Americans. We must never go back.*

*There is no room for racism, anti-Semitism, or other forms of ethnic and racial hatred in this country.*

—RONALD REAGAN

*Believing as we did that the war was a war of subjugation, and that it meant, if successful, the destruction of our liberties, the issue in our minds was clearly drawn. . . . The Union without Liberty, or Liberty without the Union.*

— Randolph Harrison McKim,
*A Soldier's Recollections:*
*Leaves from the Diary of a Young Confederate,* 1910

The past is not dead. It isn't even past.

—William Faulkner

*The Civil War defined us* as what we are and it opened us to being what we became, good and bad things . . . It was the crossroads of our being, and it was a hell of a crossroads . . . We think we are a wholly superior people. If we'd been anything like as superior as we think we are, we would not have fought that war. But since we did fight it, we have to make it the greatest war of all times. And our generals were the greatest generals of all time. It's very American to do that.

—Shelby Foote,
*on why Americans are drawn to the Civil War,*
*quoted in* The Civil War, *Ken Burns, 1990*

I subscribe to William Faulkner's view that history is not just about what we were before but who we are now.

—Ken Burns

For every Southern boy fourteen years old, not once but whenever he wants it, there is the instant when it's not yet two o'clock on the July afternoon in 1863, the brigades are in position behind the rail fence, the guns are laid and ready in the woods and the furled flags are already loosened to break out and Pickett himself with his long oiled ringlets and his hat in one hand probably and his sword in the other looking up the hill waiting for Longstreet to give the word and it's all in the balance, it hasn't happened yet . . .

—William Faulkner,
*Intruder in the Dust*, 1948

*War means fighting. The business of the soldier is to fight. Armies are not called out to dig trenches, to throw up breastworks, to live in camps, but to find the enemy and strike him; to invade his country, and do him all possible damage in the shortest possible time. This will involve great destruction of life and property while it lasts; but such a war will of necessity be of brief continuance, and so would be an economy of life and property in the end.*

—C.S. LIEUTENANT GENERAL THOMAS J. JACKSON, quoted from G. F. R. Henderson, *Stonewall Jackson and the American Civil War*, 1995

*The South may not be always right, but by God it's never wrong!*

—"BROTHER" DAVE GARDNER

We ask no gifts, no charities, but simply our rights for which we have fought and bled in your armies, and for which so many of our noblest men have died. We make our earnest appeal to the President of the United States and to Congress. We entreat you to regard sacredly your past treaties with us, and to enact no law that shall sweep out of existence those most sacred rights which you have guaranteed to us forever.

— The 1866 Cherokee Delegation

*We did not fight to perpetuate human slavery,* but for our rights and privileges under a government established over us by our fathers and in defense of our homes.

—C.S. Colonel Richard Henry Lee

*Truth crushed to the earth is truth still*
*and like a seed will rise again.*

—JEFFERSON DAVIS

We must remember the majority of southerners did not own slaves and most certainly did not fight so others could own them. The real answer is quite simple. *The South was fighting because it was invaded.*

—FRANCIS W. SPRINGER

*Duty is ours; consequences are Gods.*

—C.S. LIEUTENANT GENERAL THOMAS J. JACKSON, QUOTING JOHN QUINCY ADAMS

*The Southern rebellion was largely the outgrowth of the Mexican War. Nations, like individuals, are punished for their transgressions. We got our punishment in the most sanguinary and expensive war of modern times.*

—Ulysses S. Grant,
*Personal Memoirs of U. S. Grant,* 1885

*I have fought against the people of the North* because I believed they were seeking to wrest from the South its dearest rights. But I have never cherished toward them bitter or vindictive feelings, and I have never seen the day I did not pray for them.

—Robert E. Lee

HE POSSESSED every virtue of the great commanders, without their vices. He was a foe without hate; a friend without treachery; a private citizen without wrong; a neighbor without reproach; a Christian without hypocrisy, and a man without guilt.

—B. H. HILL,
*"The Character of Lee," address before the
Georgia branch of the Southern Historical Society,
Atlanta, Georgia, February 18, 1874*

I THINK THAT LEE SHOULD HAVE BEEN *hanged. It was all the worse that he was a good man and a fine character and acted conscientiously. It's always the good men who do the most harm in the world.*

—HENRY BROOKS ADAMS

*D*o your duty in all things . . . You cannot do more; you should never wish to do less.

—ROBERT E. LEE

I believe throughout his life Jefferson was dedicated to his conception of what America was and ought to be. He considered himself an absolutely loyal patriot. The Confederacy in his mind was an attempt to save what he considered the legitimate America. *He considered himself and his fellow Confederates to be the true descendants of the founding fathers.*

—WILLIAM J. COOPER,
*on Jefferson Davis*

*I worked night and day for twelve years* to prevent the war, but I could not. The North was mad and blind, would not let us govern ourselves, and so the war came.

—JEFFERSON DAVIS

*The enduring realization that when a great challenge comes, the most ordinary people can show that they value something more than they value their own lives. When the last of the veterans had gone, and the sorrows and bitterness which the war created had at last worn away, this memory remained.*

—BRUCE CATTON,
*on the legacy of the Civil War*

# THE RIGHT OF REVOLUTION
## IS AN INHERENT ONE.

*When people are oppressed by their government, it is a natural right they enjoy to relieve themselves of the oppression, if they are strong enough, either by withdrawal from it, or by overthrowing it and substituting a government more acceptable. But any people or part of a people who resort to this remedy, stake their lives, their property, and every claim for protection given by citizenship—on the issue.*

*Victory, or the conditions imposed by the conqueror—must be the result.*

—ULYSSES S. GRANT,
*Personal Memoirs of U. S. Grant,* 1885

...THEY TRIED TO MAKE
my uncle Harrison into an informer, but he wouldn't
do it. He was only a boy ... They tried to hang him,
time and again they tried it, "stretching his neck",
they called it, but he didn't say anything. I think
he'd have died before he'd said anything. He's the
one I'm named after. And I'm happy to say that
there were people around at the time who said I
took after him.

—PRESIDENT HARRY S. TRUMAN,
*speaking about what the Yankee "Redlegs" did to his uncle,*
*at age thirteen during the "War Between the States"*

*You may be whatever you resolve to be.*

—THOMAS J. JACKSON,
NOTE QUOTED FROM HIS PERSONAL JOURNAL

*I think we continually need to understand* how important an event the war was—how defining, how central to who we are . . . Even now there's an echo of the war, however faint, in almost everyone's life.

—KEN BURNS

*For 134 years the American people have been led to believe that the right of secession had been overturned by a "verdict of arms," but that isn't true . . . It is true the shot fired at Fort Sumter was a mistake since it provided the pretext for the Southland to be invaded by foreign troops, but the right of secession realized through the ballot box remains an essential part of our constitutional order.*

—GEORGE KALAS

As soon as slavery fired upon the flag it was felt, we all felt, even those who did not object to slaves, that slavery must be destroyed. *We felt that it was a stain to the Union that men should be bought and sold like cattle.*

—Ulysses S. Grant,
*comment to German Chancellor Bismarck*
*on his trip around the world, 1878,*
*quoted in William S. McFeely,* Grant: A Biography, *1982*

The American people,
North and South, went into the war as citizens of their respective states, they came out as subjects . . . what they thus lost they have never got back.

—H. L. Mencken

# WE HAVE MUCH TO SAY IN VINDICATION OF OUR CONDUCT, BUT THIS WE MUST LEAVE TO HISTORY.

*The bloody conflict between brothers, is closed, and we "come to bury Caesar, not to praise him." The South had $2,000,000,000 invested in Slaves. It was very natural, that they should desire to protect, and not lose this amount of property. Their action in this effort resulted in War. There was no desire to dissolve the Union, but to protect this property.*

## *The issue was made and it is decided.*

—STERLING COCKRILL,
PLANTER FROM COURTLAND, AL,
LETTER TO PRESIDENT ANDREW JOHNSON,
SEPTEMBER 18, 1865

*T*he Principle for which we contend is bound to reassert itself, though it may be at another time and in another form.

—Jefferson Davis

Experience proves that the man who obstructs a war in which his nation is engaged, no matter whether right or wrong, occupied no enviable place in life or history. Better for him, individually, to advocate "war, pestilence, and famine," than to act as obstructionist to a war already begun.

—Ulysses S. Grant,
on antiwar activity, *Personal Memoirs of U. S. Grant*, 1885

THE PRINCIPLE, ON WHICH THE WAR WAS WAGED BY THE NORTH, WAS SIMPLY THIS: *That men may rightfully be compelled to submit to, and support, a government that they do not want; and that resistance, on their part, makes them traitors and criminals. No principle, that is possible to be named, can be more self-evidently false than this; or more self-evidently fatal to all political freedom.*

*Yet it triumphed in the field, and is now assumed to be established.*

—Lysander Spooner

*We could have pursued no other course without dishonor.* And sad as the results have been, if it had all to be done again, we should be compelled to act in precisely the same manner.

—Robert E. Lee

**NOTHING FILLS ME WITH DEEPER SADNESS** *than to see a Southern man apologizing for the defense we made of our inheritance. Our cause was so just, so sacred, that had I known all that has come to pass, had I known what was to be inflicted upon me, all that my country was to suffer, all that our posterity was to endure, I would do it all over again.*

—JEFFERSON DAVIS

*It will be a glorious day for our country* when all the children within its borders shall learn that the four years of fratricidal war between the North and South was waged by neither with criminal or unworthy intent, but by both to protect what they conceived to be threatened rights and imperiled liberty: that the issues which divided the sections were born when the Republic was born, and were forever buried in an ocean of fraternal blood.

—C.S. LIEUTENANT GENERAL JOHN B. GORDON

I SAW IN STATES' RIGHTS THE
only availing check upon the absolutism of the sovereign
will, and secession filled me with hope, not as the destruction but as the redemption of Democracy. . . . Therefore I deemed that you were fighting the battles of our
liberty, our progress, and our civilization, and I mourn for
the stake which was lost at Richmond more deeply than
I rejoice over that which was saved at Waterloo.

—LORD ACTON,
*letter to Robert E. Lee right after the war*

*I* *n our government-controlled schools we are taught
that Lincoln was our greatest president because his
war ended slavery and saved the Union. As usual, the
other side of the story—the side that reflects poorly on
the government—somehow gets lost.*

— RICHARD J. MAYBURY,
*The Abe Lincoln Hoax*

*Governor, if I had foreseen the use* those people designed to make of their victory, there would have been no surrender at Appomattox Courthouse; no sir, not by me. Had I foreseen these results of subjugation, I would have preferred to die at Appomattox with my brave men, my sword in this right hand.

—Robert E. Lee,
*comment to Governor Fletcher S. Stockdale*
*of Texas, August 1870*

*Only at the moment when Lee handed Grant his sword was the Confederacy born; or to state matters another way, in the moment of death the Confederacy entered upon its immortality.*

—Robert Penn Warren,
*"The Legacy of the Civil War," 1961*

*The pageant has passed. That day is over.*
*But we linger, loath to think we shall see them no more*
*together — these men, these horses, these colors afield.*

—JOSHUA LAWRENCE CHAMBERLAIN

ENGRAVE UPON THE HEARTS OF . . . ALL THE young men of our commonwealth the remembrance of the patriotic valor, the loyalty to truth, to duty, and to God, which characterized the heroes around whose remains we weep, and who surrendered only to the last enemy . . . *death.*

—REVEREND DR. MOSES HOGE,
*prayer for the Confederate dead of Gettysburg,*
*June 20, 1872*

*In the South the war is what AD is elsewhere;*
*they date from it.*

—MARK TWAIN,
*Life on the Mississippi*

—

*S*trange, *(is it not?) that battles, martyrs, blood,*
*even assassination should so condense — perhaps*
*only really lastingly condense — a Nationality.*

—WALT WHITMAN

—

*I hope the day will never come* that my grandsons will
be ashamed to own that I was a Confederate Soldier.

—C.S. PRIVATE A. Y. HANDY

# Before the war

it was always the United States *are*, after the war
it was the United States *is* . . . it made us an is.

—Shelby Foote,
quoted in *The Civil War*, Ken Burns, 1990

# The Civil War is, for the American

imagination, the greatest single event of our history.
Without too much wrenching, it may, in fact, be said
to *be* American history. Before the Civil War we had
no history in the deepest and most inward sense. . . .
It became a reality, and we became a nation, only with
the Civil War.

—Robert Penn Warren,
*The Legacy of the Civil War:*
*"Meditations on the Centennial,"* 1961

*Civil war is a terrible crucible* through which to pass character; the dross drops away from the pure metal at the first touch of fire.

—C.S. Commander Raphael Semmes,
*Memoirs of Service Afloat*, 1868

*Were these things real? Did I see those brave and noble countrymen of mine laid low in death and weltering in their blood? Did I see out country laid waste and in ruins? Did I see soldiers marching, the earth trembling and jarring beneath there measured tread? Did I see the ruins of smoldering homes cities and deserted homes? Did I see the flag of my country, that I had followed so long, furled to be no more unfurled forever? Surely they are but the vagaries of mine own imagination . . . But hush! I now hear the approach of battle. That low, rumbling sound in the West is the roar of cannon in the distance.*

—Sam Watkins

*It will be difficult to get the world
to understand the odds against which we fought.*

—ROBERT E. LEE,
LETTER TO JUBAL A. EARLY, MARCH 15, 1866

I always thought the Yankees had something to do with it.

—GEORGE E. PICKETT,
*when asked why the Confederates were defeated at Gettysburg*

THE ASSERTION
that the South fought for slavery is Yankee propa-
ganda and a monstrous distortion . . .

—JEFFERSON DAVIS

FUTURE YEARS WILL NEVER KNOW THE *seething hell and the black infernal background, the countless minor scenes and interiors of the secession war; and it is best they should not.*

*The real war will never get in the books.*

—WALT WHITMAN,
*"The Real War Will Never Get in the Books,"* 1882

*As a Southerner I would have to say* that one of the main importances of the War is that Southerners have a sense of defeat which none of the rest of the country has.

—SHELBY FOOTE,
quoted in *The Civil War*, Ken Burns, 1990

*Everyone from the South knows who Jefferson Davis was, and this is one thing that distinguishes the South from other parts of the country.*

—WILLIAM F. BUCKLEY

EVERYONE SHOULD DO ALL IN HIS POWER TO collect and disseminate the truth, in the hope it may find a place in history and descend to posterity. History is not the relation of campaigns, and battles, and generals or other individuals, but that which shows the principles for which the South contended and which justified her struggle for those principles.

—ROBERT E. LEE

*In war, men are nothing, a man is everything.*

—NAPOLEON BONAPARTE

*I think the most interesting personality I ever encountered was General Grant. How and where he was so much larger than other men I had ever met I cannot describe. It was the same sort of feeling, I suppose that made my friend, Thomas Starr King, whilst listening to a celebrated preacher, turn to me and exclaim, "Whereabouts in that figure does that imperial power reside." You had that feeling with Grant exactly.*

—MARK TWAIN,
interview in Sydney (Australia), *Morning Herald*,
September 17, 1895

# Lee was an aggressive

general, a fighter. To succeed, he knew battles were to be won, and battles cost blood, and blood he did not mind in his General's work. Although always considerate and sparing of his soldiers, he would pour out their blood when necessary or when strategically advisable.

—C.S. Brigadier General Gilbert Moxley Sorrel, *Recollections of a Confederate Staff Officer*, 1905

*Grant's whole character* was a mystery even to himself—a combination of strength and weakness not paralleled by any of whom I have read in Ancient or Modern History. . . .

— William Tecumseh Sherman, *on Ulysses S. Grant*

THE ACTUAL SOLDIER OF 1861–65, NORTH and South, with all his ways, his incredible dauntlessness, habits, practices, tastes, language, his fierce friendship, his appetite, rankness, his superb strength and animality, lawless gait, and a hundred unnamed lights and shades of camp, I say, will never be written.

—WALT WHITMAN,
*Specimen Days*, 1882

*If I ever disown, repudiate, or apologize* for the Cause for which Lee fought and Jackson died, let the lightnings of Heaven rend me, and the scorn of all good men and true women be my portion. Sun, Moon, Stars, all fall on me when I cease to love the Confederacy. "'Tis the cause, not the fate of the Cause, that is glorious!"

—C.S. MAJOR R. E. WILSON

*All wars are boyish,* and *fought by boys.*

—HERMAN MELVILLE,
*Battle Pieces,* 1866

—

I DO NOT HOLD WAR
to mean simply that lines of men shall engage each other in battle, and material interests be ignored. This is but a duel, in which one combatant seeks the other's life; war means much more, and is far worse than this.

—U.S. MAJOR GENERAL PHILIP H. SHERIDAN,
*Personal Memoirs of P. H. Sheridan, General United States Army,* vol. 1, 1888

*Every time I look at Atlanta I see what a quarter million Confederate soldiers died to prevent.*

—JOHN SHELTON REED

THEY WERE SIMPLY AFRAID TO GO HOME
AND FACE THEIR WOMEN.

—GORDON COTTON,
FORMER SLAVE, ON WHY THE CONFEDERATE ARMY
FOUGHT ON WHEN DEFEAT WAS CERTAIN

**WAR IS AT BEST BARBARISM.** . . . Its glory is all moonshine. It is only those who have neither fired a shot, nor heard the shrieks and groans of the wounded, who cry the aloud for blood, more vengeance, more desolation.

*War is hell.*

—U.S. LIEUTENANT GENERAL
WILLIAM TECUMSEH SHERMAN,
SPEECH AT THE MICHIGAN MILITARY ACADEMY,
JUNE 19, 1879

*War loses a great deal of romance after a soldier has seen his first battle. I have a more vivid recollection of the first than the last one I was in. It is a classical maxim that it is sweet and becoming to die for one's country; but whoever has seen the horrors of a battle-field feels that it is far sweeter to live for it.*

—C.S. COLONEL JOHN S. MOSBY

THE SOUTHERNERS were fighting with the energy of despair, hoping that some untoward event might spring up to help them. At all events, they were determined to command the enemy's respect for their courage and ability, and I don't think any brave sailor or soldier ever withheld it.

—U.S. ADMIRAL DAVID D. PORTER,
*Incidents and Anecdotes of the Civil War*, 1885

One of the noblest duties of the living is to *perpetuate the virtues and memories of the dead.*

—C.S. Brigadier George Gordon,
*dedication of a monument to Major General
Patrick R. Cleburne, Helena, Arkansas, May 10, 1891,
Southern Historical Society Papers*

Every battlefield of the Civil War beheld the deadly conflict of former friends with each other. . . . If we had to be beaten it was better to be beaten by former friends. Every true soldier loves to have "a foeman worthy of his steel." Every true man likes to attribute high qualities to those who were only friends, though now alienated for a time. The temporary estrangement cannot obliterate the recollection of noble traits of character.

—C.S. Major General Daniel H. Hill,
*Battles and Leaders of the Civil War*, vol. 2, 1888

## THE LOST CAUSE IS THE CONFEDERACY.

*It is referred to as the Lost Cause . . . Lost things are always prized very highly. The South conducted itself bravely in an extremely difficult situation. Many of the things we're proudest of in the American character were exemplified in the southern soldier, for instance.*

*We take a justifiable pride in the bravery of those men, North and South.*

—SHELBY FOOTE,
QUOTED IN *The Civil War,* KEN BURNS, 1990

*That old man . . .* had my division massacred at Gettysburg.

—GEORGE PICKETT,
*comment to John S. Mosby shortly after paying Lee a visit in Richmond, March 1870*

*The war for our Union, with all the constitutional issues which it settled, and all the military lessons which it gathered in, has throughout its dilatory length but one meaning in the eyes of history. It freed the country from the social plague which until then had made political development impossible in the United States. More and more, as the years pass, does the meaning stand forth as the sole meaning.*

—William James, 1897

*Well, it made you immortal.*

—John S. Mosby's reply to Pickett

THE CIVIL WAR WAS REALLY ONE OF THOSE watershed things. There was a huge chasm between the beginning and the end of the war. The nation had come face-to-face with a dreadful tragedy . . . And yet that's what made us a nation. Before the war, people had a theoretical notion of having a country, but when the war was over, on both sides they knew they had a country. They'd been there. They had walked its hills and tramped its roads . . . They knew the effort that they had expended and their dead friends had expended to preserve it. It did that.

The war made their country an actuality.

—SHELBY FOOTE,
*The Civil War*, Ken Burns, 1990

I WOULD NOT HAVE the anniversaries of our victories celebrated, nor those of our defeats made fast days and spent in humiliation and prayer; but I would like to see truthful history written. Such history will do full credit to the courage, endurance and soldierly ability of the American citizen, no matter what section of the country he hailed from, or in what ranks he fought. . . . As time passes, people, even of the South, will begin to wonder how it was possible that their ancestors ever fought for or justified institutions which acknowledged the right of property in man.

—U.S. LIEUTENANT GENERAL ULYSSES S. GRANT

**In great deeds something abides.**

On great fields something stays. Forms change and pass; bodies disappear, but spirits linger, to consecrate ground for the vision-place of souls. And reverent men and women from afar, and generations that know us not and that we know not of, heart-drawn to see where and by whom great things were suffered and done for them, shall come to this deathless field to ponder and dream; And lo!

*The shadow of a mighty presence shall wrap them in its bosom, and the power of the vision pass into their souls.*

—U.S. Major General Joshua L. Chamberlain, dedication speech at Gettysburg for a monument to the 20th Maine, October 3, 1889

*T*hrough our great good fortune, in our youth our hearts were touched with fire. It was given to us to learn at the outset that life is a profound and passionate thing. While we are permitted to scorn nothing but indifference, and do not pretend to undervalue the worldly rewards of ambition, we have seen with our own eyes, beyond and above the gold fields, the snowy heights of honor, and it is for us to bear the report to those who come after us. But, above all, we have learned that whether a man accepts from Fortune her spade, and will look downward and dig, or from Aspiration her axe and cord, and will scale the ice, the one and only success which it is his to command is to bring to his work a mighty heart.

—OLIVER WENDELL HOLMES JR.,
*Memorial Day Address, May 30, 1884,*
*at Keene, New Hampshire*

And when the wind in the tree-tops roared,
The soldier asked from the deep dark grave:
"Did the banner flutter then?"
"Not so, my hero," the wind replied.
"The fight is done, but the banner won,
Thy comrades of old have borne it hence,
Have borne it in triumph hence."
Then the soldier spake from the deep dark grave:
"I am content."
Then he heareth the lovers laughing pass,
and the soldier asks once more:
"Are these not the voices of them that love,
That love—and remember me?"
"Not so, my hero," the lovers say,
"We are those that remember not;
For the spring has come and the earth has smiled,
And the dead must be forgot."
Then the soldier spake from the deep dark grave:
"I am content."

—Oliver Wendell Holmes, Jr.,
*poem quoted in his speech, "The Soldier's Faith,"*
*Memorial Day Address, May 30, 1895, Harvard University*

# INDEX

Porter, David D., 68, 199, 284
Porter, James D., 190
Potter, Andrew, 62
*Providence Journal*, 165

**R**
Reagan, Ronald, 250
Reed, John Shelton, 282
Reynolds, John F., 141
Rhodes, Elisha Hunt, 81, 135, 155
Rosecrans, William S., 120
Russell, William Howard, 63, 231

**S**
Sedgwick, John, 176
Semmes, Raphael, 274
Seward, William H., 52
Shaw, Robert Gould, 139
Sheridan, Philip H., 172, 179, 281
Sherman, John, 100
Sherman, William Tecumseh, 14,
    100, 158, 180, 183, 185, 186, 187,
    192, 194, 199, 279, 283
Smith, Edmund Kirby, 104
Smith, Goldwin, 165
Smith, Gustavius W., 96
Sorrel, Gilbert Moxley, 279
Spooner, Lysander, 267
Springer, Francis W., 256
Stanton, Edwin, 213
Stephens, Alexander H., 17, 44, 198
Stockdale, Fletcher S., 270
Stowe, Harriet Beecher, 109, 160, 244
Stuart, J. E. B., 104, 128, 166, 179

Sumner, Charles, 247
Swinton, William, 203

**T**
Tocqueville, Alexis de, 3, 48
Thompson, David L., 105
Thoreau, Henry David, 40
Toombs, Robert, 53
Trimble, Isaac R., 93
Trobriand, Regis de, 126
Truman, Harry S., 262
Tubman, Harriet, 41
Twain, Mark, 49, 246, 272, 278

**V**
Vallandigham, Clement, 239
Vincent, Strong 144

**W**
Wakefield, J. S., 235
Warren, Robert Penn, 270, 273
Washington, Edward L., 177
Washington, George, 228
Watie, Stand, 210
Watkins, Sam, 65, 175, 191, 207, 274
Waugh, William Archibald, 146
Welles, Gideon, 98
Whitman, Walt, 161, 241, 225, 272,
    276, 280
Wightman, John T., 46
Williams, J. C., 119
Wilson, R. E., 280
Wise, Henry A. Jr., 200
Wright, Horatio 102